Fifty Years a Runner

*My Unlikely Pursuit of a Sub-4 Mile
and Life As a Runner Thereafter*

William Blewett

Copyright © 2023 William Blewett

No part of this book may be reproduced, scanned or distributed without permission.

All rights reserved.

ISBN: 9798375637136

TABLE OF CONTENTS

Chapter One: "If I faltered" 1
Chapter Two: Got started, got shoes, got lapped 6
Chapter Three: Into the mileage trap 15
Chapter Four: Overmatched 22
Chapter Five: Hard, easy, hard lessons about damage and repair 26
Chapter Six: Twenty-six-mile detours 31
Chapter Seven: "You're not finished, young man." 38
Chapter Eight: Aerobic, anaerobic and Arthur Lydiard 45
Chapter Nine: Cunningham, Ryun and the Steamroller 51
Chapter 10: Psyching up, not out 57
Chapter 11: Well-aimed poison arrows 62
Chapter 12: Imperfect workouts 67
Chapter 13: Interval training and the heart 74
Chapter 14: The trouble with doubles 87
Chapter 15: The phenomenon of running like a deer 96
Chapter 16: What I didn't know: how to rise from a plateau 104
Chapter 17: What I neglected: rebuilding leg and hip strength 112
Chapter 18: Catch-as-catch-can training and road racing 118
Chapter 19: No immunity from bad luck 126
Chapter 20: Venous valves and booster pumps 132
Chapter 21: Fear of death on the run 137
Chapter 22: Roger Bannister should have been my role model 145
Chapter 23: My long post-racing decline 149
Chapter 24: How my running came to an end 160

Dedication

This book is dedicated to J.D. Martin, who in his second year as cross-country and track coach at the University of Oklahoma, accepted me as a freshman walk-on even though I had never bettered 5 minutes in the mile. J.D. went on to coach for 23 years at OU and to be inducted into the Oklahoma Sports Hall of Fame, and I, thanks to his patient coaching, became the runner I dreamt of becoming.

Fifty Years a Runner

William Blewett

Chapter One

"If I faltered"

There is a tide in the affairs of men.
Which, taken at the flood, leads on to fortune;
Omitted, all the voyage of their life is
bound in shallows and in miseries.

It has been more than a half-century since I memorized this passage from Shakespeare's *Julius Caesar* in twelfth-grade English class. I did so in the same year I went out for high school track in the Great Plains city of Lawton, Oklahoma. Seven years after I first stepped on the track, these words rose from my memory at a decision point in what had become a long and unlikely pursuit of a dream.

It was the most memorable of many decision points I reached in my running career. Every athlete surely comes to such a point at least once, whether in a nascent career—being cut from a junior high school sports team—or in a long, storied career of Olympic greatness. Should I continue to chase this dream? This was my question in 1972, as I prepared to run a race that seemed likely to lead on to fortune. Should I continue the toil of running two workouts a day, six days a week aimed at becoming a sub-4 miler, maybe even an Olympian? Or should I allow my zeal for athletics to default to spectatorship?

A British medical student named Roger Bannister delivered a memorable statement of his own as he approached a similar decision point in May, 1954. In his autobiography,[1] he described his feelings just before he made headlines around the world for running the first sub-4-minute mile in history.

* * *

"The arms of the world were waiting to receive me if only I reached the tape without slackening my speed. If I faltered, there would be no arms to hold me and the world would be a cold, forbidding place, because I had been so close."

He had already decided that the 1954 season would be his last in pursuit of the sub-4 mile. It was his eighth season since he entered Exeter College, Oxford and had run a personal best mile of 4:53.0 as a freshman. At age 25, he was in medical school, preparing to fully immerse himself in a career as a physician. He was a brilliant man, who in no way would spend the rest of his life bound in shallows and miseries if he failed to break 4 minutes.

On May, 19, 1972, I reached what I thought would be my Roger Bannister moment on a track in Pasadena, Texas, a suburb of Houston. I had graduated from the University of Oklahoma a year earlier and had begun the only job I was offered in a down year for mechanical engineering graduates, an internship as a civilian engineer with the U.S. Army near Texarkana, Texas. The time was right for checking the trajectory of my running career as it intersected with my new career as an engineer. I had run at least 20,000 miles in training over the previous seven years with only minor setbacks. I had adapted well. I was running well.

For four years I had been guided by an outstanding coach at the University of Oklahoma, J.D. Martin. After that, I coached myself while seeking to learn more of the science of runner training. I had studied how Peter Snell, three-time Olympic gold medalist and world record holder, had developed, and I had met with the coach who had guided him to fame, Arthur Lydiard. I had read about the methods of Oregon's legendary coach Bill Bowerman, who had developed more sub-4 milers than any other coach. I had studied about 200 training profiles of champion runners from around the world in Fred Wilt's books, *How They Train*. I had even run two leg-numbing workouts in California under the famous Hungarian coach, Mihali Igloi, who developed the third miler ever to break 4 minutes, Laszlo Tabori.

Among my many races, there were performances I would describe as good, ordinary, bad, or humiliating. The latter two chipped away at my spirit and resolve, clouding my dreams with doubt. Occasionally, however, an unexpected phenomenon would visit me and lift my spirits by transforming what would have been an ordinary race into a painless, personal-best performance. Lacking a better description, I began to think of this as *running like a deer*. This was not a second wind. It was more like a personal tailwind, pushing me 360 degrees around the track. It would counteract any effect of The Bear, the mythic creature born of lactic acid that would intrude as a shoulder passenger to produce painful, slow-motion running near the finish.

Looking back at my detailed training logbooks, I count little more than a dozen races in which I ran like a deer, a small number compared to the times I suffered through a bell lap with The Bear on my back. Though these races were few, I learned from the book *Psychocybernetics*, that in pre-race warmup, I should rerun in my mind the races in which I had run like a deer. This mental exercise seemed beneficial but not quite adequate for my desired result. It did indicate that the phenomenon was physiological, more so than psychological.

The most memorable of these was the mile race I was preparing to run in the Meet of Champions in Houston on a pleasant spring evening. At the time I did not understand this phenomenon or know when to expect its benevolence. I had never read anything about it. Now, having had 50 years to study it, I can finally explain it, and will do so in this book.

Seven years to reach my goal of sub-4 seemed about right. From the time Bannister first broke 5 minutes in the mile, he needed seven more years of training and racing to run the first sub-4 mile in history. He did that in 1954, when I was a first-grader oblivious to his remarkable achievement. His Australian contemporary, John Landy, needed seven years to improve from 4:58.0 to 3:58.0. He became the second man to break 4 minutes, also in 1954. I broke 5 minutes with a 4:58 in my first week of cross-country in college in the fall of 1965. I later plotted my year-to-year progression in the mile against theirs, and it aligned well. Extrapolation indicated that I would break 4 minutes as well.

The conditions for my race in Houston were near perfect—75 degrees with a wind of just 2 to 3 mph—and in this meet the previous two years, I had run personal bests of 4:04.8 and 4:04.5.

In track races, hearing lap splits helps a runner maintain the desired pace. My splits on that evening in Houston were 60 seconds for the first lap, 61 for the second, and 63 for the third. The third lap was too slow, but I was relying on Texas Southern University star Tommy Fulton to set the pace. I ran two yards behind him until the gun lap, but when he kicked the last quarter mile in 57.6, I responded with a

58.1. He finished in 4:01.4, which at the time was the second fastest mile ever run in the State of Texas. I finished in 4:02.1.

I had run like a deer. I wasn't fatigued at the finish. I never felt The Bear, and I recovered very quickly. If the pace had not slowed in the third lap, I might have run 4:01, or even 4:00.

It wasn't the result I sought, but I looked at the bright side of my performance. I had run a new personal best by 2 ½ seconds. By just 3 tenths, I had missed the meet record set by Cary Weisinger, who formerly held the American record in the mile at 3:56.6. Though I was no longer an NCAA athlete, I had bettered the OU school record of 4:03.6 held by the great South African runner Gail Hodgson. And I had finished close behind Fulton, a rising star who would run 3:57.8 one year later. I reminded myself that I was only 24, and that I had to keep training for one or two more years to break 4:00. Bannister had run his celebrated 3:59.4 just a year after running a personal best of 4:02.0

Surely that was plenty of time to drop another 2 ½ seconds. I knew, however, that my quest could become not just a race against the stopwatch but a race against the calendar, knowing that the inevitable decline that results from the wear and tear of intense training might hasten the time when there would no longer be a next time, when there would be no reclaiming the power of youth no matter how assiduously I trained.

It was, of course, impossible to predict the future. I never considered how many years I would give myself to reach this goal before settling into a sedentary life. Perhaps, like Bannister, I would retire from racing after breaking 4 minutes, or perhaps I would retire short of my goal and never gain a full understanding of the requisites for success in running the mile.

Seven years in, I still had much to learn, and I seemed to learn at a slower rate than the questions about training and racing arose. I was still ignorant of how to bring myself reliably to peak readiness for each race. I had not solved the mystery of running like a deer. I had not learned to find my personal optimal intensity of training and racing, and I knew not how to discern sound training advice from the harder-is-always-better recommendations of other runners. Bannister and Landy faced a similar challenge—learning by trial and error how best to train as the science of runner training gradually emerged in the early 1950s.

As Bannister and Landy probably did years earlier, I relied on the expertise of outstanding coaches and sound medical science—not on folk science. My training may have placed me among the most dedicated of milers, but as the saying in athletics goes, there will always be someone faster to come along. That person may have more natural ability or apply superior knowledge of science in training. My lack of knowledge led me to make many mistakes.

Even though my story begins half a century ago when sub-4 miles were few and infrequent, I believe it holds valuable lessons for any runner seeking to become faster. Runners of any era begin with the same approach as I, taking advice from anyone who offers it, and making the same mistakes I made. Learning how to train seems even more difficult than training itself.

Fifty years ago, the science of exercise physiology was advancing rapidly. Though it offered the potential for better training methods, it was not being widely applied by coaches and athletes to achieve optimal runner training. Races in the twenty-first century are largely the same as they were 50 years ago. Also unchanged are the physiology and anatomy of the human body, the adaptations that build power and energy efficiency, and the competitive nature of people. Some things have changed in 50 years, of course: the tracks, the culture in the realm of running at each level, perceptions of how hard to train and how often to race, and the willingness to submit to the off-the-track requirements of training—particularly proper sleep and nutrition. The spirit to excel remains unchanged, as does the difficulty in finding one's own personal best intensity of training.

I learned much in my first seven years of racing. Unfortunately, the knowledge most important to my reaching full potential came to me *after* the end of my racing career. My quest to run sub-4 became a quest to learn more of the science of runner training merely for lifelong fitness. I did not conceive that my quest would continue into my seventies.

What is the key to becoming a champion runner? What did I do right? What did I do wrong? How should I have trained? What follows is the story of my 57 years as a runner, a lifelong adventure in developing and sustaining my power and efficiency as a runner, with training that was (in order), intuitive, empirical, and scientific. It was a longer journey than I ever predicted it would be.

Chapter Two

Got started, got shoes, got lapped

When I was 17 and mostly interested in learning to fly airplanes, I resolved to do something in athletics few people had ever done—to run the mile in less than 4 minutes. This was just 11 years after Roger Bannister famously became the first man to break the 4-minute barrier in London. In the 11 years that followed, only 14 Americans bettered 4 minutes. When I decided upon this ambitious goal, I knew of only one of the 14—Jim Ryun, a Kansas schoolboy my age, who because of his youth, was to become as famous as Bannister.

In that Olympic year, Ryun's story was presented to the world, and to me in Lawton, via television, newspapers, and magazines. He was what I dreamed of becoming – fast and famous. If for some reason I could not be like Ryun, I wanted to be like Billy Mills, the University of Kansas alumnus who won the 10,000-meter gold medal in the 1964 Olympics. Ryun rose from obscurity to worldwide fame in just two years. Mills rose from obscurity to Olympic gold in the span of 28 minutes, the time it took him to win the 10,000 meters. I watched his Olympic victory on our Philco TV. It was stunning, even in fuzzy black and white.

I was an inveterate dreamer then. I dreamed of flying, and at 17, I built a biplane hang glider with a 20-ft wingspan for $22 from an article I found in a 1909 *Popular Mechanics* magazine in Lawton's Carnegie Public Library. When I finished the glider, my brother Tom and I carried it two miles to a gently sloping hill in Elmer Thomas Park, a place in which I had many times flown control-line model airplanes. When I attempted to fly the glider, I was fortunate in being unsuccessful. I say fortunate because I had no knowledge of how to land it without breaking a leg. By extension, it was not outrageous to believe that I could make another of my daydreams reality—that I could ascend to Olympic fame in middle-distance running, even though I had never even run a mile without stopping. My unwritten sports resume then included retirement from little league baseball at age 11, one unremarkable season of peewee football at age 12, and at 13 being cut from the junior high basketball team after a 10-minute tryout.

At 14, I decided to run a time trial one summer afternoon to check my reservoir of latent ability and reduce the uncertainty of my future in athletics. I ran what I figured was a mile on a gravel road near my home. My course was a straight line from our neighborhood, Sneed Acres, to Dewey Shaw's Market, a small grocery store on Fort Sill Blvd. I figured it had to be a mile, because I could barely see the store from my starting point. I prepared my wrist watch and took off at what I thought was an appropriate pace. I reached the store breathless and fatigued in 5 minutes and 20 seconds, only 81 seconds slower than Roger Bannister's best mile. It was a performance that neither encouraged nor discouraged me until the odometer of our family car revealed a few days later that I had run only seven-tenths of a mile. There was still no reason to believe I possessed any latent talent for athletics.

I Set an Unofficial Record in Football

The next step in the search for my yet-unquantified athletic talent was to try high school football. In August of 1964, I was one of 120 boys who went out for the Lawton High School Wolverines. I began on the lowest rung, tenth-string fullback, of a very good team, which had in its backfield Eddie Hinton who later starred for the Baltimore Colts of the National Football League, and Rick Baldridge, who later started at fullback for the University of Oklahoma. I brought to this challenge a large amount of spectating experience accrued in front of our Philco. In watching college football, I became a fan of Fearless Frankie Solich, the quick, elusive All-Big-8 Nebraska fullback who weighed 153 pounds. I aspired to be like him because he weighed just five pounds more than I did, and he was a star. He was, for a brief period, my role model.

As my rookie football season progressed, I rose to fourth team fullback, mostly through roster attrition, but I soon realized I was no Frankie Solich. In the first game of the season, with our team leading a clearly inferior Elk City squad, 21-0, with 3 seconds remaining in the game—I can still visualize vividly the big, bright 00:03 on the scoreboard clock—the coaches apparently agreed that it was safe to send me into the fray at right cornerback. I trotted onto the field to the musical chant from the student section: "We are the Wolverines, the mighty, mighty Wolverines!" I was mighty, mighty scared that I might screw up. The coaches' prescience in this decision of where to place me was, however, remarkable. Elk City ran a sweep to the left side, *not to my side*. It was a sweep that went for naught. The shutout was preserved. In those 3 seconds, I went from being a sideline spectator to an on-the-field spectator, then back to the sideline. I never again got into a game, in fact never again stood on the sideline in full regalia and readiness. My complete football career lasted only 3 seconds, which surely would have been an Oklahoma high school record for brevity, except that no one noticed.

I tell about my initial failures in sport because I believe the script is generally the same for many young athlete-wannabes who end up on the track or cross-country team, where their success is not heavily dependent upon the opinion of coaches or the abilities of teammates. There is the popular belief too that running sports are democratic ones, in which each person can succeed based on amount of time and effort put in on training. This is only half true at best.

I Found My Niche in Sports

In the early spring of 1965, I went out for track and knew instantly that I had found my place in sports. I ran one season, competing in the half mile (880-yard) run and the mile relay. I won only one race, but that win sparked a fire of enthusiasm within me. It came in the 880 in the Boomer Conference Championships, held in Lawton in May 1965. It was the most thrilling and encouraging race of my career. It was my first time to experience running like a deer, though I did not realize it at that time. I won with a strong kick in 2:01.7, coming from fourth-place, 10 yards behind in the final 50 to nip the lead runner in the last step. The finish was so exciting it seemed almost as if it were staged for a movie. When I crossed the line, at least a dozen students, none of whom I knew personally, rushed out of the stands and crowded around me in celebration. It was as if I were Roger Bannister and I had just run the first sub-4 mile. They didn't go so far as to lift me onto their shoulders, but I never again experienced such a celebratory finish. If this is what winning a track race is like, I thought, I'm eager to win more.

When I was warming up for the race with my six-transistor radio in hand, I heard a beautiful instrumental song I had never heard before, *Wonderland by Night* by Bert Kaempfert. It was captivating and soothing. As a neophyte knowing nothing about "psyching up," I assumed it to be a clear message from the heavens that I was to win. I did win. Buoyed by success, I purchased the 45-rpm record and played it at home many times before each of my next two track meets. The song's potency, however, had apparently expired shortly after my win. I was winless in the last two races of my high school season, the regional and state meet. I was, however, ready for what I perceived would be an exciting and rewarding journey in track.

The common belief among runners and coaches was, and still is, that if you weren't a state champion with outstanding performances in high school, you had no chance of making the track team at a Division 1 university, and you surely could not become a sub-4 miler. No one informed me of these prerequisites, so three months after the season ended, I packed a suitcase, some corrugated boxes, and a load of aspirations and rode with my parents 90 miles to the City of Norman to enter the University of Oklahoma.

Jim Ryun's Arrival Was Noteworthy. Mine Was Not

The first task in my ascent into college athletics was to find the track locker room in the southeast corner of the cavern beneath Owen Field, the Sooners' football stadium, which had a capacity of 55,000 fans. About the same time, a freshman named Jim Ryun was arriving at the University of Kansas with great fanfare and quite different circumstances. He was the most precocious miler of the twentieth century, perhaps of all time. He was a high responder of the highest order, which means that he improved with training at a phenomenal rate. As a high school sophomore, he improved from the back of the pack in fall cross-country to a 4:07.8 mile in the spring of his first year of running, roughly five times more quickly than Bannister and Landy improved. He made the U.S. Olympic team as a high school junior and broke the American record in the mile with a 3:55.3 before he arrived at KU.

To ensure that Ryun would continue breaking records as a member of the Jayhawks' track team, the University dismissed its very successful, long-time coach, Bill Easton, so it could replace him with Bob Timmons, the coach who guided Ryun's ascent to world prominence at Wichita East High School. This coaching change was the final step in clearing the way to bring the 17-year-old star to KU. In the next four years, Ryun did not disappoint KU or the State of Kansas, unless his silver-medal finish in the 1,500 meters at the 1968 Olympic Games qualifies as a disappointment. Before he won the medal, he set world records in the mile, 1,500 meters, and 880 yards, and an American record in the 2-mile.

Unheralded, Unimpressive, and Almost Unwanted

In contrast to Ryun's arrival in Lawrence, Kansas, my first appearance at the OU track locker room in the same month was unheralded, unimpressive, and almost unsuccessful. I wandered into it on a 100-degree September day and asked coach J.D. Martin if I could be on the cross-country team. This was not an act of courage; it was an act of naivete. I didn't even consider that he might say no because I believed, without any supporting evidence, that I would become an outstanding runner. He could have easily said no.

In a normal year, he probably would have said no, but as I later learned, this was to be a deficient season for the OU cross-country team. There were no returning standouts, and only three freshmen had been recruited. J.D. was looking for fresh talent, but as I stood before him citing my best performances—a 2:01.0 half mile and 51.6 quarter mile on the mile relay—he did not perceive that helpful talent was close at hand. "Okay, you can come out for the team, but I can't give you any running shoes," he said, apparently thinking I would quickly transition from walk-on to drop-out. I did not know what a walk-on was, but I was pleased to have become one.

Two weeks later, after he had watched me run several interval workouts at the front of the pack, J.D. presented me, without ceremony, a new pair of Adidas Oregon flats. My workouts in Lawton over the summer had produced small miracles in increasing my aerobic power. I had run one solo time trial during the summer, a 36:33 six-mile on the track in 90-degree heat, to prove to myself that I could run longer distances.

Obsessed with becoming a champion miler, I began to read *Track and Field News*, a periodical that had long touted itself as "The Bible of the Sport." Although I read it religiously, I never understood the Bible analogy. *Track and Field News* was presented more like a thin version of the Lawton phone book with its many pages and long columns of performance lists. I studied each issue cover to cover, much more intently than I read my differential equations textbook. I would compare my times, which were not good enough to be listed until 1970, with other collegiate runners in the U.S. Doing so was, however, a routine of discouragement, convincing me that I was clearly a tail-ender and that trying to become a competitive runner was a waste of my time. With the effort I was investing in workouts, I was essentially majoring in track and cross-country and minoring in engineering. Either I shouldn't have tried to become a collegiate runner, or I shouldn't have been reading *Track and Field News*.

I persisted in reading it, however, probably for the same reason some people persist in watching horror movies despite knowing that fright is sure to engulf them. I was also filled with self-doubt as I got further into the Big-8 competition against Olympians, national champions, conference champions, and a soon-to-be world record holder, Jim Ryun. I kept my focus, however, on the daily workouts, in which I was showing steady improvement. Improvement is the engine for improvement, I would tell myself, and this kept me going, even after the embarrassment of being hugely overmatched in the Big-8 freshman mile in Kansas City, just six months after I rejoiced in breaking 5 minutes in the mile for the first time.

Lapped in Kansas City

The banked board track in the Kansas City Municipal Auditorium was small, only 146 yards around, 12 laps to the mile, which ensured that in running against the world's best miler, almost everyone in the race would receive a public shaming—being lapped by Jim Ryun. Motivated by a deafening roar from the 10,000 spectators who had come only to see him break 4 minutes, Ryun sought to please. He finished in 3:59.6, three quarters of a lap ahead of the second-place runner.

I was proud that I had improved my mile time to 4:27 three weeks earlier. Pete Carney, my teammate who was also in the race, had a best mile time of about the same. We didn't need a calculator or slide rule to predict we would be lapped. Pete, who ran so effortlessly that J.D. sometimes accused him of loafing, had two questions about the race, one before and one after. Why was Ryun running against us ordinary freshmen—I think the word he used here was peons—when he should have been running against other world-class milers? His question afterwards, which he bellowed upon seeing that *The Daily Oklahoman* newspaper had covered the race and mentioned by name that Pete and I were the first two runners lapped, was: "why? Why the hell did they have to mention that?" I believe that I, not Pete, was actually the first runner lapped, but we did not quibble about who should claim this distinction. Being lapped in the mile is an unusual, perhaps unique, occurrence in a major college meet, but the conditions and competition were just right for this humiliation.

I tried to repress the memory of the race. Pete apparently was unable to do so. He kept a mental ledger of poor races and discouraging workouts. Two years later he quit the team. Like Pete, I thought often about quitting in my freshman year. I always became extremely nervous before races. In warming up I would ask myself, why am I doing this? If the race went well, my answer would be: "because I love it." If it went poorly, my answer would be: "I should quit. Why submit to torture and public humiliation?"

Everything A Young Runner Would Want To Be

Jim Ryun probably inspired thousands of youngsters to become distance runners—and a similar number to quit trying to be distance runners. He was everything a young runner wanted to be but couldn't be. He was ultra-famous. He appeared on the cover of *Sports Illustrated* seven times and was known throughout the world. But he and his coach created a cultural shift in training methods that surely had negative effects on the development of many young runners. That is, he trained far harder than other middle-distance runners, and his killer workouts were well known. For example, when he was 16, he ran 40 x 440 yards one day during a 110-mile week. His best-known workout was 20 x 440 in 60 seconds each.

In being the first teenager to break 4 minutes, he probably influenced runners worldwide to try to do so, but he did not create a flood of sub-4 high schoolers as one might expect. After he broke 4 minutes and made the U.S. Olympic Team in 1964, two others did so in the next three years—Tim Danielson in 1966 and Marty Liquori in 1967. Then, there were no others for 34 years. Alan Webb of Virginia broke the drought in 2001 and went on to break several of Ryun's records, but not to achieve his greatness.

Coach Timmons became well-known for his discovery. At the time, however, it was uncertain just what he discovered. Was it the holy grail of runner training, the series of workouts he applied to Ryun and other Wichita East High School runners, which could turn virtually any healthy young male into a sub-4 miler? Or did he simply discover the world's most resilient, most rapidly adapting runner, the highest of high-responders?

Timmons' coaching record eventually indicated it was the latter. From among the many promising runners drawn by Ryun's success to join the KU track team during Timmons' 24-year tenure as the head coach, he developed only one sub-4 miler, and that was Ryun. In contrast, Bill Bowerman, who applied a uniquely thorough understanding of training methods at the University of Oregon, developed 16 sub-4 milers in his 25 years as head coach.

Excessively hard runner training still persists in the twenty-first century, thanks in part to Timmons and Ryun. It seems to be widely employed by college coaches as a means of culling prospects who are not high responders in what could be called the recruit-and-cull approach to developing great track teams. Runners like Roger Bannister and John Landy might not develop quickly enough for a four-year, NCAA Division 1 college program and probably would not have had a chance to do so in the Ryun era. High school coaches also employ culling, whether knowingly or not, in following the trend of the college coaches. In high school track, overly hard training is especially counter-productive relative to the goals at that level.

Science later indicated that rapid development such as Ryun's was not due simply to running exceptionally hard workouts. Regarding high responders, the book, *Physiology of Sport and Exercise* [2] states: "Heredity largely explains individual variations in response to identical training programs. It is clear that this is a genetic phenomenon, not a result of compliance or non-compliance (with training)."

Is It Heredity Or Training?

As a novice inspired by Ryun's success, I initially believed it was both the training and heredity, but I later realized that in Ryun's case, it was mainly heredity. Every runner is unique in the combination of attributes that determine rates of recovery and growth in the cycles of work and rest to bring about the important adaptations. The problem was that I did not know this when I needed to know it, nor did I know my own in-born ability. The issue of how hard to train is one countless runners and coaches have addressed over many years. Hippocrates, the father of modern medicine, touched on it 25 centuries ago when he wrote:

> *"The right amount of nourishment and exercise, not too little, not too much, is the safest way to health."*

To modern-day coaches and runners, health means being injury free and adapting successfully in training. Modern-day physicians know the broader scope of Hippocrates' postulate; that is, for anything that is essential or beneficial to good health—exercise, food, sleep, water, oxygen, sunlight, medicines, salt, etc.—there is an optimal dose that varies from person to person over time. Too much of any good thing can be toxic. This is true of training. To improve as a runner requires the right balance of work and rest specific to each runner—optimal doses of aerobic running, anaerobic running, and resting.

Even though I had begun to improve rapidly under coach J.D. Martin, it wasn't as rapidly as Ryun had improved under Timmons. Looking back, I incorrectly assumed my slower development was due to training methods rather than genetics. So, at the end of my freshman year, I made a strategic decision about the training I would perform over the next three summers when I would be home from college. I would be bold and apply my own eclectic coaching methods, never considering that it could turn out to be less than ideal in quantity and quality for a yearling runner. I would follow the high-mileage, intense-interval-training path taken by Ryun and other world-record-setters, about which I actually knew very little. Looking back, I realize it was not a good decision.

Chapter Three
Into the mileage trap

In the summer after my freshman year at OU, I fell into a trap I had created. I call it a mileage trap. I became ensnared in it when I changed from intuitive training to empirical training.

Intuitive training is believed to be the original, natural way humans developed greater endurance and speed when they began to run 2 million years ago. It is also the type of training with which I prepared to go out for football in the summer I turned 17. I knew nothing about building endurance, so intuitive training was the logical choice. I did not know anything about it or what it was called. There was no requirement for pace or distance or duration—just run until it hurts, then slow down or walk. I had no coach. There were, of course, no coaches in prehistoric times either to guide the first human runners, and there was no language with which an observer/heckler could convey the message: "pick up the pace, you laggards. Make it hurt! No pain, no gain!"

The pioneers of running probably began by alternately walking and jogging—like beginners' fartlek or the novice workouts described in Bill Bowerman's 1967 best seller, *Jogging* [3], which I read and admired for its wisdom 40 years after its publication. Walking and jogging is believed to be the way primitive hunters developed endurance in a mode of hunting, called persistence hunting—wearing down an animal until it could be taken down with stones and clubs. This may have been the only way to acquire meat before the bow and arrow and the stone-tipped spear were invented.[4]

Guided by pain, the protective signals of the body, intuitive training is a listen-to-your-body method, self-directed by feelings or sensations without conscious reasoning to determine how fast and how far to run and when and how long to rest. In running fast for too long, pain emanates from fast-twitch muscles as they produce lactic acid and accumulate lactate or the protons that are stripped from the lactic acid in becoming lactate. Fatigue (the depleting of energy stored within the muscle fibers), overheating, dehydration, muscle microtrauma, and injury produce pain that differs in quality, intensity, speed of onset, and speed of recovery.

Empirical training

Fartlek, a free-play workout of varying speed, similar to interval training but based on how a runner feels, is a mixture of intuitive and empirical training.

With empirical training, which was first employed by the Greeks for the ancient Olympic Games, workouts were developed through observation, experience, and experimentation—testing methods that showed promise for improving speed and endurance. Empirical training became popular in the twentieth century and has been prevalent since.

Fred Wilt's book *How They Train* could be considered a primer on empirical training for distance runners. Published in 1959, it lists details of the workouts, races, and best performances of 157 champion runners (155 men and two women) from around the world. The reader can pick a runner of a certain ability and try his or her workouts. There is little mention of intuitive training in the book, although John Landy reported on his page: "I personally prefer to be guided by intuition".

In empirical training, the implication is that pain is not always an acceptable reason to slow down, that completing a workout the coach prescribes is more important than slowing down, shortening it, or skipping it due to any one of the several forms of discomfort. If pain is deemed not relevant, the message to the uninformed runner is that *if* you can complete, for example, the workouts Jim Ryun completed, you may eventually set a world record. Not true, of course.

All Miles Are Not Equal

Weekly mileage has become a simple, widely misused gauge for empirical training. It is used, often inappropriately, for setting goals, measuring progress, predicting performance, or trying to compare one runner's potential to that of other runners. The problem with it is that *all miles are not equal*. Running anaerobically places greater stress on the body than running aerobically. For example in sprinting, a runner applies about 3.7 times his body weight in force on each leg with each step, but in jogging, only 2 times body weight.[5] Anaerobic running also depletes glycogen, the energy stored within muscle fibers, much more quickly than does running aerobically. Fast-glycolytic fibers store smaller amounts of glycogen and deplete it about 13 times faster than do the slow-oxidative muscle fibers generating aerobic power. That's why fast-twitch muscle is called fast-fatigable muscle.

Speed workouts and most interval workouts are run at or above the anaerobic threshold, when the fast-glycolytic muscle fibers are activated to supply anaerobic power for the faster pace; consequently, fatigue occurs more rapidly. Also, glycogen is subsequently restored very slowly, normally in one to two days, or longer. So, recovery generally takes much longer in running above the anaerobic threshold.

Aside from the pace of the workout, other variables that determine how a person responds to training are mechanical efficiency; how, how long, and how often rest is taken; muscle-fiber mix; level of lactate steady state; level of fatigue; hydration; foot mechanics; adaptability; durability; and resilience. Environmental factors such as hills, footing, temperature, and humidity, also affect the inequality of miles.

Consequently, training cannot be adequately characterized with a two- or three-digit number that implies that more is better—that to become a better runner one must simply run more miles per week. Mileage goals can lead to forced progression in training—rather than natural progression—creating a mileage trap, a condition in which the body demands rest, and the workout plan says *no resting for you*, not until the workout plan calls for rest.

Bill Bowerman, the venerable coach at the University of Oregon, knew all this perhaps better than any coach. He knew about the tendency of young runners to go big on mileage, and he knew that as a coach, he shouldn't allow his runners to be drawn into a mileage trap.

Bowerman's Warning to Kenny Moore About Mindless Labor

In his book, *Bowerman and the Men of Oregon* [6], Kenny Moore tells of a stern admonishment he received from Bowerman as a sophomore at the track one day after Bowerman learned he had been running extra workouts to reach 100 miles per week, despite specific instructions to the contrary.

"Are you in this simply to do mindless labor, or do you want to improve?" said Bowerman. He placed his hands around Moore's throat, drawing his forehead to his and saying: "For three weeks, you are not going to run a yard except in my sight...If I or any of my spies see you trotting another step, you will never run for the University of Oregon again."

Moore complied and within three weeks, he lowered his personal best in the two-mile from 9:30 to 8:48. He went on to become a two-time Olympian, placing fourth in the 1972 Olympic marathon.

I did not know all this about mileage and the inequality of miles in June 1966, when I finished my freshman year at OU, having improved my mile best to 4:23.9 on training that averaged 40 miles per week, of which probably one-third were at or above the anaerobic threshold. I was brimming with enthusiasm and poor judgement, obsessed with running 1,000 miles over the summer break.

Summer Running Among the Prairie Dogs

Summers of southwest Oklahoma are always hot, with a southerly wind that comes sweeping up the plain, driving the moisture out of every living thing. In the summer after my freshman year, I ran 900 miles, most of it in Lawton's Elmer Thomas Park, 300 acres of grassland that had seemingly been deeded to the prairie dogs. I would run past the prairie dog village at least four times a day and see their strict security drills unfold. The sentinel of each coterie, standing tall by a burrow entrance would bark or yip the alarm when I approached, and the family and friends, who probably numbered in the thousands, would disappear into tunnels. They multiplied and expanded their village inexorably, forcing the City of Lawton to suck hundreds of them out of their tunnels with an apparently humane vacuum-cleaner-like truck and haul them to a faraway place to likely become a nuisance to another community. Thanks to the prairie dogs' security signals, I never once stepped into one of their holes.

In my first summer break from OU, I usually ran 10 or 12 miles in the evening, six days a week. I sometimes added a wakeup workout of a 1-mile warmup with my Dad followed by 4 miles easy past the prairie dogs. This training, as learned years later, had been intuitive training, guided by avoidance of pain. I ran aerobically according to how I felt. The morning pace was usually 8:00 to 8:15 per mile, and in the evening workout, 6:50 to 7:15 per mile.

Two Summers of Inflexible Mileage Goals

If the proof of summer running routine lies in the quality of racing that follows it, these hot, lonely long runs were high in benefit. I set new personal bests in cross-country, indoor track, and outdoor track in the 1966-67 school year. Every training regimen, indeed every workout is an experiment. And the 900-mile experiment in the summer of '66 proved successful.

I improved my 3-mile cross-country times by almost a minute. In the following indoor season I lowered my mile best to 4:19.0 in a dual meet attended by the Governor of Wisconsin at the University of Wisconsin. I then lowered it again in the outdoor season in a strange but memorable race against Jim Ryun in Norman, as described in the next chapter.

My goal in the second summer, 1967, was to run 100 miles a week. I had read that Ryun was running this amount and that Arthur Lydiard was prescribing 100 a week under his well-known system of training. With a firm mileage goal, the training would be empirical, at least enough so to create a mileage trap.

That summer, I ran eight straight 100-mile weeks on two workouts a day, six days a week and finished with a total of 1,220 miles. Even though I took one rest day every week, by August, I wasn't fully recovering day to day. Four days before returning to OU, I apparently reached a critical point after an 18-mile day that included an interval workout of 13 x 440 in 71 to 75 seconds with a 220 jog for rest. As I noted in my running log three days and 47 miles later, my legs felt dead, and my left Achilles tendon, left hip, left knee, and right bicep were all sore. Instead of completing my self-prescribed 10 mile-run in the next workout, I limped to a halt after 6 miles. My scale of 1-to-10 assessment in my running log, a measure of how I felt, was a "2", my lowest ever. With just one more 16-mile day I would have had my ninth 100-mile week, but I couldn't run another mile. I needed two weeks of rest. Instead I took two days. Such was the inflexibility of my mileage goals.

Such mileage in summer training was apparently unusual for an OU runner, so the Sports Information Office prepared a short release that appeared in three newspapers:

> *"Bill Blewett...got so tired of seeing opponents' backsides pass him last cross-country season that he hauled off and ran 1,200 miles this summer. That's almost enough to put Blewett in the used car status. But the work paid off. Bill slimmed his four-mile time down to 20:23 this summer, four-barrel fast compared to what he used to run."*

Indeed, it did pay off. I had improved my aerobic capacity to the automotive equivalent of a four-barrel carburetor over the summer, as demonstrated by my taking another minute off my 3-mile times in cross-country. In our first meet against the University of Arkansas, I ran a personal best of 14:32 to win and lead OU to a team win. In the next week, I beat future NAIA cross-country champ Roy Oldperson of Wichita State in a shoulder-to-shoulder duel over 4 miles in Wichita. A week later I ran 14:14 for 3-miles to finish second, 8 seconds behind Pat McMahon of Oklahoma Baptist, a four-time All-American in cross-country. Another week later I set a course record in leading OU to its first win over Oklahoma State in 16 years.

In the following indoor track season, I improved my 2-mile time to 9:08.1 in finishing fifth behind Ryun (9:00.8) in the Big-8 Championships on the same 12-lap Kansas City track on which I had previously been embarrassed. In the spring, I lowered my mile best to 4:11.8 in winning the annual dual meet against Oklahoma State on a windy, 90-degree day.

Looking back on the summer training of 1967, I realized that with one rest day per week—a sort of recovery catch-up day—prepared me well for improving my performances throughout the three competitive seasons of my sophomore year. I had achieved a good, but certainly not perfect, balance between running and resting.

Perfection, however, cannot be defined by mileage numbers because, of course, all miles are not equal. It is the progression in performances and intuitive feedback indicating a balance between running and resting that defines near-perfection in training. Almost all of these summer miles were aerobic miles, and I did not recognize this in evaluating my accomplishment. I incorrectly saw it as validation that more is better when it comes to mileage, encouraging me to run greater mileage.

I did suffer a lack of recovery in August. It became apparent right after I threw in an interval workout to cap a 17-mile day. There was a lesson there, about the importance of finding the optimal intensity of training. I did not learn from it. I would pay for it the following summer.

Chapter Four
Overmatched

In boxing, overmatching a novice in a fight is very bad strategy for developing a boxer. It can yield irreversible damage to the psyche. The same is true in running sports. A sound beating can bring a quick end to a budding career. Fortunately, Roger Bannister was never overmatched as he progressed through the eight years of his running career.

I faced the terror of being overmatched in Kansas City in the indoor season of 1966. It was the Big-8 freshman mile, an event that in any normal year would have been a sort of novice mile for collegians, but with freshman Jim Ryun being an American record holder, it became an extreme overmatching. Looking back and re-running the race many times in my mind, I rationalized that Ryun and I were not actually racing against each other. I had merely shared the track with him, as a golf cart might share a four-lane highway. When he had just over a lap to go, he was barreling toward a crescendo of dominance known as lapping the field. He needed me to get out of his way. I, in bewilderment, needed a rear-view mirror to do so without tripping him (God forbid). The 10,000 screaming fans would have punished me with a din of boos and hurled crumpled coffee cups into my path had I caused him to miss his sub-4-minute finish by a tenth or two. That race was a psychological body blow. Luckily, it left me with no permanent damage.

In the spring of 1967, I learned that I would be overmatched again, the second time in 15 months. This became apparent when Ryun and his University of Kansas team were scheduled to visit OU in May. For this unique occasion, I was asked to give a radio interview to publicize the OU-KU dual meet in which he and I would run on Saturday. There was no mention of Kansas City in the interview, but there was still the human-interest aspect of our matchup. OU's green-horn miler, who had recently run a personal best of 4:19.0, was preparing to run against the world record holder in the mile, who had run at 3:51.3. To ensure full stands at the meet, it was probably best to emphasize that he and I would again be sharing the track.

The track stadium at OU is named for John Jacobs, who coached at OU for 46 years. Known as Jake, he was a humorist once referred to as the Will Rogers of the red dirt track. He was around as an informal assistant coach when I was a freshman, and he kept the athletes loose with his humor. One of his Jake-isms directed at a runner who was always looking over his shoulder in races was: "don't bother looking back; there won't be anybody behind you."

That quotation briefly entered my mind as I warmed up on the day of the meet, preparing to face Ryun and two of his teammates, both of whom were rumored to be capable of 4:05 in the mile. There was a near-capacity crowd of about 3,000, and most of them had come to see the most precocious and most famous American miler in history. At least two people in the crowd had come to see the green-horn miler run: my parents. I was hoping to show them a good race, but neither they nor I knew how the race would turn out, except that I would probably come in a distant fourth.

When the starter's gun fired, I went to the lead and focused on running the pace that felt right for me. I would later write in my log book that I wasn't psyched up or nervous, and that it felt good to lead (I was always honest with my log book). I was, however, puzzled to be in the lead. I was afraid to ignore Jake's advice about looking back, but I learned that I had a 15-yard lead after one lap and a 25-yard lead after two. I was still 25 yards ahead with 1 ½ laps to go, but I soon began to hear footsteps—the ominous, rhythmic sounds of the Kansas runners' spikes crunching through the cinders behind me.

They caught up with me just before the end of the third lap and stayed with me until we had 110 yards to go. Despite my best kick, they passed me and spread from a file to a rank formation, side by side, crossing the finish line in a three-way tie at 4:14.6. There were a few scattered boos from the stands, directed not at me but at Ryun, who in my estimation was the least likely runner in the world to be booed. Some spectators must have felt they were entitled to see a sub-4-minute mile or at least preternatural burst of speed at the end. I finished in 4:15.6 and immediately received congratulations from many people, which increased my puzzlement, since only the first three places scored points, and I had finished fourth. The meet concluded with Kansas winning, 74-71. Had I finished second, we would have won.

Frank Boggs, columnist for *The Daily Oklahoman*, apparently sensed that the crowd was perplexed that Ryun failed to meet expectations. Out of duty as a prominent sports writer, he would explain the mystery with a Sunday morning column under the headline, "Ryun can run just like anybody else." Appearing with the column was a rather large photo of me with my mouth open wide to facilitate repayment of my oxygen debt.

"Everybody Was Busy Congratulating Bill Blewett."

Mr. Boggs' lead paragraph was, "It really would have been pretty funny Saturday if the judges had peered across the finish line and determined that Jim Ryun blew it and Bill Blewett won it." Mr. Boggs went on to explain that Ryun was just running to win so that his team would win the meet. He did not use the word ordinary, but for Ryun it was one of several ordinary races he had to run in dual meets. He concluded the column with: "Anyhow, when Saturday's mile race was over, everybody was busy congratulating Bill Blewett. And rightly so. He tried awfully hard."

Actually, it was not an awfully hard race for me, because this turned out to be one of my rare running-like-a-deer performances. I didn't feel pain and I pushed the pace the whole way to a new personal best. I figured I was ready to run even faster the following weekend when the Big-8 Conference Championships would be held at OU.

For Ryun, the Big-8 meet would mean two more ordinary races, first in the mile and then the 880, which he was expected to win to ensure the Jayhawks could reclaim the team title from the Nebraska Cornhuskers, which they did. This was probably what his coach called "training through the meet" to prepare for more important upcoming races.

Ryun was good enough to train through and win comfortably. I wasn't, and I had not learned how to taper properly for races. Tapering means reducing the intensity of the workouts leading up to the race to bring about full recovery by race day. Full recovery means that glycogen is completely restored to the muscles that power the run. It also means that muscle damage that occurs routinely in running, particularly in races, is fully repaired, and that the runner rehydrates well enough to fully restore blood volume.

Advancing to The Rear

Recovery is uncertain when races are as frequent as one per week. Years later I learned from the work of Dr. David Costill of the Ball State University Human Performance Lab, that there is a reduced rate of glycogen storage after eccentric exercise (running) that induces delayed onset muscle soreness.[7] My calf muscles were always sore the day after a mile race. Unfortunately, my performance in the Big-8 meet was probably a demonstration of this effect. I was still thinking that two easy days would be enough time to achieve full recovery for the race. I did not understand that deficits of glycogen, tissue repair, and even hydration can become cumulative. I had to consider what I had done in the previous two weeks: I ran a mile race on May 4, another on May 9, then my personal best against Kansas on May 13. In addition, I ran six anaerobic workouts, so on nine of the 15 days preceding the Big 8 meet, I had run anaerobically.

Ryun won the Big-8 mile in a tactical 4:08.5. Expecting to run like a deer again, I led the race for the first 2 1/4 laps at a pace that was very close to what I had run eight days earlier. Once I gave up the lead, I began advancing to the rear of the pack and at some point in the last lap, a heavy ursine passenger climbed aboard and slowed my pace almost to a jog. I finished 14th out of 16. *The Daily Oklahoman* extended my period of undeserved celebrity by publishing a photo taken about a quarter mile into the race, when I was leading.

If you were to look closely at the photo you would see my nostrils flaring as I reached the quarter mile mark in 60.5 seconds not feeling at all fleet-footed as I had a week earlier. That photo would years later inform me about how residual fatigue had affected my mechanics and mechanical efficiency. It would reveal something I had missed and help explain why I did not run like a deer that day but instead lugged The Bear.

Chapter Five

Hard, easy, hard lessons about damage and repair

Two huge display boards were mounted high on the walls of the OU track locker room. On one wall was the runner's creed, and on the opposite wall, the track and field school records. The creed, which probably originated with Ken Doherty, the venerable coach of the University of Pennsylvania, read like this. "I will win. If I cannot win, I will place. If I cannot place, I will run, throw or jump better than ever before."

One day, I noticed that the creed had been altered with white athletic tape cleverly covering selected words and letters. It read: "I will win. If I cannot win, I will throw up." No one ever took credit for the modification, but the Sooner track teams needed neither version as a reminder to run hard. As novice runner, I was awed by the stellar athletes who wore the OU singlet, present and past. Rarely, if ever, did I see anyone coast to the finish line, not in workouts and certainly not in races.

A Cautionary Tale About Interval Training

I often studied the school-record board, imagining that one day my name would be listed there. What first caught my attention was the record for the outdoor mile, 4:03.6 by Gail Hodgson, and the indoor mile, 4:12.4 by George Brose. I never met Gail, who came to OU from South Africa, but I did meet George years later when he and I both had slowed to jogger status.

George was recruited by OU coach Bill Carroll in 1961 from Dayton, Ohio. He was the Ohio state record holder in the mile, having run

4:20.0 to break the old record by 4 seconds his senior year. His goal, like mine, was to break 4 minutes in the mile, and he progressed well through his junior year at OU when he ran 4:09.8 in the mile and placed third in the 1,000-yard run in the Big-8 indoor meet behind future Olympian Tom Von Ruden of Oklahoma State University. George worked ever harder in interval workouts each year at OU, adding more repetitions, reducing the rest periods, and increasing the speed. In January through May of his senior year, the routine he set for himself was to run four intense interval workouts—usually 220s, 440s, 880s or 1320s—Monday through Thursday each week followed by only one rest day before a track meet on Saturday.

This routine led him not to new personal bests but to the breaking point of his career. "I was dead meat on the hoof that year, psychologically worn out as well," he told me. "I just couldn't push myself anymore." In his workouts, George should have eased off and coasted more. His best time as a senior was 4:17.

George's experience is one of several cautionary stories of overtraining on interval I have heard over the years. Unfortunately, I didn't learn from them before the summer of 1968.

In that summer, my last before my collegiate eligibility ended, I increased the intensity of my training routine much like George did with his. Recognizing the benefits of interval, I believed that it would be good to add three interval workouts per week while still running a total of 100 miles per week. It would have been better if I had greatly reduced my mileage, but like George, I was on fire to continue improving, so I did not do so.

How Bill Bowerman Coached Interval

It is best to run interval training with at least one easy day, perhaps two, after each interval-workout day. I did not learn this until much later when I read the book *The Bowerman System* by Chris Walsh, which describes Bill Bowerman's coaching principles and workouts in detail. [8] A routine of alternating hard days and easy days facilitates recovery and reduces the stress, particularly on the lower legs, which are very susceptible to injury.

Bowerman prescribed two easy days after each hard day for runners like Kenny Moore, who he perceived did not recover as well as the others. The easy days were for recovery and were indeed easy. The complete workout was not to exceed 20 minutes: for example, 1 to 3 miles of jogging and some weight-lifting or swimming. For most of Bowerman's runners, the routine was hard-easy-hard. For high responders like Steve Prefontaine, however, it was hard-hard-easy, that is two hard days followed by one easy day.

My easy days in the summer involved aerobic running, fairly easy in pace but not so easy in distance with the effects of heat stress and dehydration in the mid-90s heat that prevailed in the late evenings in Lawton. On those days, I usually ran 16 miles—6 in the morning and 10 in the evening. The pace in the evening was 6:40 to 7 minutes per mile.

Igloi's Indirect Influence

My hard interval day workouts came to me from an issue of *Track and Field News*, which carried an article about Tracy Smith, a member of the 1968 U.S. Olympic team in the 5,000 meters. He was a former high school star in California who ran a 9:11.0 two-mile and a 4:12.6 mile as a prep. He later bettered the world record for the 3-mile indoors three times, solidifying it at 13:07.2. A disciple of coach Mihali Igloi, Smith ran interval workouts of short repetitions such as 40 x 220 with a 220 jog after each. Two years later I did a couple of workouts under Igloi and learned that for him, 40 x 220 would be considered a light workout.

I decided to add the 40 x 220 to my summer-of-'68 training and resolved to run it three times each week. The result: my cycles were hard-harder-hard. This was a problem, even though I rested one day a week, I was digging a hole, a deficit of recovery for my lower legs. Looking back, I wish I had someone that summer who would place his hands around my neck, lift me partially off the ground and tell me sternly to cut this craziness out. Here was a typical training week.

> Monday, AM: 1.5-mile jog warmup, 6-mile run at 7:30/mile pace. PM: 1.5-mile warmup, 40 x 220 in 31-33 with 110 jog after each. 1.5-mile cool down.
> Tuesday, AM: 1.5-mile jog, 6-mile run at 7:15/mile pace. PM: 10-mile run at 6:40 pace
> Wednesday, AM: 1.5-mile jog, PM: 1.5-mile warmup, 40 x 220 in 32-34 sec. with 110 jog. 1.5-mile cool down.

Thursday, AM: 1.5-mile warmup, 6-mile run at 7:30 per mile pace, PM: 10-mile run at 6:55 per mile pace.
Friday, AM: 6-mile run at 7:20 per mile pace. PM: 1.5-mile warmup, 40 x 220 in 31-33 sec. with 110 jog. 1.5-mile cool down.
Saturday, AM: 8-mile run at 7:15 per mile pace. PM: 8-mile run at 6:59 per mile pace.
Sunday, Rest

There was a second problem. I ran the 220s in spiked track shoes with long spikes on a hard, dry cinder track. This placed more stress on my calves and Achilles tendons, and before long, without a true recovery day or two, active or otherwise after each interval workout, I had a full-blown case of inflammation in both Achilles tendons. Being obsessed with running 100 miles a week, however, I did not respond with the logical remedy—taking time off to heal. I wouldn't even allow myself two consecutive days off; taking a month or two off was beyond my comprehension. I stuck to the routine for 13 weeks despite the soreness. The result: I had chronic pain in both tendons that would persist for almost 20 years. To paraphrase Ben Franklin: experience keeps a dear school, but overzealous distance runners will learn in no other.

Summer of 1968 Turning Point

The Achilles injury in the summer of 1968 might have been a turning point in my pursuit of 4 minutes. I kept improving, but run-like-a-deer races became less frequent. The soreness would diminish slowly then return suddenly after a race or hard workout, making it difficult to taper properly. It did, however, force me to lighten my training more before races, that is, to taper better. The cyclic nature of the soreness was apparent in my two races in the Peachtree 10K in Atlanta. I won the Peachtree in 1973, in the normally oppressive Fourth-of-July heat and humidity of Georgia. Two years later, when my right Achilles was very sore on race day, I placed twenty-eighth, with a time almost 2 minutes slower than I ran in 1973, even though I managed to run much faster for the first 3 miles of the race (14:25). Except for the Achilles soreness, I was probably in much better racing shape in the 1975 race, as evidenced by the personal bests at 2 miles and 3 miles I ran off lighter-than-usual training that involved less anaerobic running.

In 1968, however, the Achilles injury was not my only adversity in training. There was one other important setback that summer. I ran a marathon.

Chapter Six

Twenty-six-mile detours

A historic Olympic race crept into my daydream as I ran a workout one day in preparation for my first marathon, the 1968 U.S. Olympic Trials. I had read about Emil Zatopek, the Czech star who won four Olympic gold medals, one in 1948 and three in 1952. The story of how he won his fourth gold medal in 1952 intrigued me. After winning the 5,000 and 10,000, he decided at the last hour to run the marathon. He was the world record holder at the 5,000 and 10,000, but he was a novice, a first-timer in the 26-miler, a race that presents much harsher challenges than the 5,000 or 10,000.

His lack of marathon experience was apparent in the first half of the race. Running beside Jim Peters, the favorite from Great Britain, he asked Peters twice near the 10-mile mark if the pace was about right. The second time, Peters replied that it was too slow, when actually it wasn't. Zatopek took the lead soon thereafter but struggled, holding back with what he described as an irresistible urge to give up near the halfway point. He held on to win by over 2 minutes in 2:23:04, suffering greatly. Peters, who led the race through much of the first half, dropped out from heat exhaustion about six miles from the finish.

Dreaming I Could Be Like Zatopek

Knowing about his first-time success, I fantasized that I might be in a position to do at age 21 what Zatopek had done at age 30, completely ignoring the fact that the trials would be held at high altitude. My flawed reasoning was that I had been running 100 miles a week; I had a mile performance equivalent to Zatopek's 1,500-meter best; and I had run many long interval workouts over the previous three years (he was the unmatched master of interval training, known to have run 100 x 400 in 75 to 90 seconds in a single day many times.)

There was no specific qualifying time for the 1968 Olympic Trials marathon, nor was there a requirement to have run a marathon previously. To enter, I had to submit for review my personal bests in shorter races. Because the Games would be held at Mexico City's 7,382 feet elevation, the U.S. Olympic Committee held the marathon trials in Alamosa, Colorado, elevation 7,544 feet.

Physiologists had determined that to run well in the thin air of Alamosa, one had to have been at that altitude for at least 30 days, or less than 24 hours before the race. It was a matter of either acclimating or avoiding the initial, negative effects of becoming acclimated.

My father and I planned the trip to be there less than 24 hours. On August 17, we drove the 550 miles from Lawton in 9 hours in my Volkswagen Beetle.

The Lesson of One Leg At a Time

There were plenty of stars in the field of 119 starters. I noticed two of them as I entered a small restroom in the gym of Adams State College before the race—Billy Mills, 1964 Olympic gold medalist in the 10,000 meters and George Young, who would eventually compete in four Olympic Games and win the bronze medal in the steeplechase in 1968.

The ventilation system of the restroom was apparently not designed to handle the heavy load of vaporous products of pre-race anxiety worthy of an Olympic marathon trial. I remember it as a overwhelming stink. I respectfully did not attribute the offensive odor to these two Olympic stars but to the many other runners who passed through beforehand. I was reminded of something my high school track coach, Don Jimerson, once said to allay the fears of facing superior competitors. "They put their pants on one leg at a time, just like you do." A corollary for the marathon trials then crossed my mind: They get nervous and stink up a restroom just like you do. Like most of my pre-race thoughts, however, neither of these strengthened me psychologically for the race.

All the entrants had good reason to be nervous and not just because three spots on the Olympic team were at stake. There was much uncertainty about dehydration and how performances would be affected by the thin air. Fifty-six of the 119 starters, including Mills, did not finish the race. The drop-out rate, however, wasn't a true measure of its difficulty. Everyone was affected differently by the high altitude, and no one, for sure, was running for a personal best time. Most were running to place in the top three, and there was no point in finishing once the likelihood of doing so diminished. My friend Pat McMahon, a student at Oklahoma Baptist University, whom I had raced against in cross-country, led much of the race before dropping out at 22 miles, saying that his pace was much too fast for the altitude. He had already been named to the Irish Olympic team, so there was no point in continuing. He later placed twelfth in the Olympic marathon in Mexico City.

I set a conservative pace, just as Zatopek had done in his marathon, but my daydream of winning or qualifying as a first-timer dissipated somewhere in the first mile, which I completed in 5:38, far back in the pack. I ran the second mile in 6:10 and the third in 6:00. In the last 21 miles, I passed 48 runners—nothing better to do but count them—even though I slowed down to a 7:35 per mile pace with stomach cramps in the last 5.2-mile lap. I finished in 2:53:46 in 26th place. George Young won in 2:30:48. Kenny Moore was second in 2:31:47.

Only Six Small Cups of Gatorade

Every runner was weighed in and weighed out, with the eminent exercise physiologist Dr. David Costill recording the data. I lost eight pounds over the relatively flat course, dropping from 152 to 144, which was initially surprising since it was a breezy 72 degrees at the 3 p.m. start. I learned, however, that the greater solar load and a lower atmospheric pressure at the high elevation caused sweat to evaporate more rapidly. Consequently the problem was not primarily overheating but dehydration, loss of blood volume and the diminished aerobic power resulting from the diminishing blood volume as the race progressed. The six small cups of Gatorade I drank during the race, were completely inadequate.

I learned a lot about the marathon that day, mainly that dehydration is a serious problem. A second important lesson was revealed afterwards: recovery does not occur quickly. It took two months to fully recover from that marathon. How did I know this? By comparing my times and level of effort in workouts before and after, and the "dead" feeling in my legs. Why does it take so long? It is the muscle damage that naturally occurs in running as the leg muscles lengthen against their force (eccentric contraction) with each stride. The debris from the extensive muscle damage can overwhelm the kidneys, slowing the repair process. The muscle damage is probably worsened by dehydration and depletion of the primary fuel, glycogen, after about 20 miles, with fat taking over as the fuel and providing a lower level of power. Once fatigue sets in, the heels drop, reducing the shock-absorption ability of the Achilles tendons, increasing the road shock and the resultant damage.

Such effects occur to all marathoners. When Zatopek finished his first and only marathon, it would be a week before he could walk normally. "The bounce had been hammered out of his calves and thighs. The next day he had to hobble downstairs backwards. 'My legs were hurting up to my neck,'" according to his aptly named biography, *Today We Die a Little*.[9]

If one does not take the time to recover completely from a marathon with active rest such as jogging or running easy aerobic workouts, muscle damage can accumulate and result in muscle loss. The fast-twitch muscles are most susceptible to damage because of their thinner Z-disks, the bulkheads spaced every 2 microns in the myofibrils, to which the biological springs called titin are attached. Fast-twitch muscle (fast oxidative glycolytic) provides a small portion of the power in a marathon, but this portion can provide the decisive difference.

Jim Peters' Disastrous Marathon of 1954

I learned all of this—and the story of Jim Peters' second marathon disaster—long after my marathoning was done. Peters, who collapsed from heat exhaustion in the Olympic marathon Zátopek won, collapsed again in the 1954 British Commonwealth Games in Vancouver, in the same stadium 45 minutes before Roger Bannister outran John Landy to win the Miracle Mile. The world's best marathoner at the time, Peters, held a 17-minute lead when he entered the stadium to run a final 400-meter lap in front of 35,000 spectators, who were ready to cheer his triumph. His entrance, however, drew gasps not cheers when the effects of his too-fast early pace, bright sun, and 83-degree heat became apparent.

Peters did not drink even a sip of water during the race. He preferred cooling himself with a wet sponge. But water applied to the skin does not restore lost blood volume, so he steadily lost aerobic power during the race. It was as if he were powered by an electric battery that gradually ran down until his legs would neither move nor hold him erect any longer. Even the second-place runner, British teammate Stan Cox, 17 minutes behind Peters, suffered a heat injury. He ran into a telegraph pole at 24 miles and failed to finish.

British sportswriter Peter Wilson, who watched from the press box, described Peters' attempt to finish: "Two steps forward, three to the side. So help me, he is running backwards now....Oh, he's down again....The nauseous spectacle of a semi-conscious man being allowed to destroy himself while no one had the power or gumption to intervene." After 11 minutes of staggering and falling, he fell for the last time 220 yards short of the finish line and was given life-saving medical aid. Unconscious for three hours, he was said to be near death in the hospital, where Roger Bannister, who had recently been certified as a doctor, attended to him. He recovered but never raced again.[10]

With the importance I placed on becoming faster at the mile, I should have sought to learn more about the hazards of the marathon before going to Alamosa. I did not, and I did not learn about Jim Peters' experience before I ran my second marathon two years later in Artesia, New Mexico. In it, I experienced heat stress and dehydration; fortunately this did not advance as far as Jim Peters' breakdown did.

My Near-Disastrous Artesia Marathon

The 1970 Artesia Marathon was conducted over a point-to-point course which began 26 miles from downtown Artesia. It was a generally straight course for as far as the eye could see with only a short "S" turn through high plains desert at 3,800 ft elevation. The elevation dropped 500 feet over the 26.2 miles, so it was a fast course in cool weather. Pat McMahon proved that when he won it in 2:19:49 on a much cooler day in 1968, the year he finished second in the Boston Marathon and twelfth in the Olympic marathon. I believe he recommended the race to me. I recommended it to no one.

In some ways my race went like Jim Peters' last marathon, adjusted for altitude. I began at a pace faster than I should have, reaching the 10-mile point in 57:40. On the last day of February, in what should have been cool weather, the temperature was 75 degrees, which in direct sun is warm for marathoning. Like Peters, I was deficient at drinking. There were supposed to be four water stops, but two were not set up in time, so I took only two cups of ice, a half cup of water and three orange slices in ignorance of the urgency to hydrate. The inadequacy of this became apparent after 12 miles, a mile after I took the lead, and about the time I felt the initial effects of heat injury. I believe I stopped sweating at 17 miles then developed dizziness, fatigue, dead legs, abdominal cramps, and nausea. But since this was not an important race and my lead was about 3 miles, I slowed the pace when these symptoms appeared and finished in 2:51:25, eight pounds lighter than my weight at the start. I later wrote in my log book that the last 1.5 miles were unbearable.

The nausea persisted past the finish, and I feared that I might stain the meet director's dress shoes with the remnants of my pre-race meal as he presented my trophy. I had won by 20 minutes, but I felt like I had lost something.

I had been naive about the effects of the weather, which turned out to be more severe than anticipated, and about the effects of inadequate water stops along the route. I did not react well to the symptoms of heat injury that became serious nine miles from the finish. This race had zero potential benefit to my development as a miler, so I should have taken a DNF (did not finish). There would have been no shame in doing so. It became apparent that I lacked good judgement in picking my races.

Seven Weeks of Recovery Was Not Enough

The Artesia Marathon also required two months to recover fully. Seven weeks after it, I was still in recovery mode when I ran the Glenn Cunningham Mile in the Kansas Relays and finished in a very disappointing 4:13.3 with a 68-second last lap. Dave Wottle, who would win the 800-meters in the Olympics two years later, passed me with 300 yards to go as if I were walking. Six weeks after that race, I finally returned to race readiness. I ran a personal best in the mile, 4:04.8 in Houston, running like a deer.

Had I been able to ask any of the great milers—Glenn Cunningham, Jim Ryun, or Roger Bannister—whether I, as an aspiring miler, should race a marathon or two, I would probably have been told: don't be so foolish. Or if my mother had voiced her thoughts upon seeing my gaunt appearance in the post-race newspaper photo, it would likely have been the same response of Joan Benoit's mother upon seeing her daughter's tortured appearance in a news photo after she won the

Boston Marathon in a world-record time: "If marathons make you look like this, please don't run any more."

Or if I had asked Emil Zatopek about running another marathon, he might have repeated what he said after his Olympic marathon victory: "If you want to run, run a mile. If you want to experience a different life, run a marathon."

Chapter Seven
"You're not finished, young man."

As the summer of 1969 began, I approached an eligibility fork in my road toward a sub-4 mile. After four years of college, I was no longer eligible to run in NCAA competition. At the same time, I became eligible to be drafted into the military. The Vietnam war was still five years from ending, and 40,000 Americans had already perished in that faraway country, so this was not a casual transition. Some of my contemporaries in the Big-8 responded in different ways.

Three OSU stars—Tom Von Ruden, John Perry, and Chris McCubbins—entered the service upon graduation and were selected for the Army Track Team, coached by recently retired OSU coach Ralph Higgins. This opportunity was offered to outstanding track and field athletes because of their potential for making the 1968 U.S. Olympic team. Von Ruden did make the Olympic Team in the 1,500. Perry, the 1966 Big-8 champion and record holder in the 880 who led OSU's 4x880 relay team to a world record, did not make the Olympic team; he went to flight school and flew combat missions in Vietnam.

McCubbins, who once patted me on the butt as he lapped me in a three-mile race at OU, was an NCAA champion and Pan-American Games gold medalist in the steeplechase. He narrowly missed making the U.S. team for the modern pentathlon. He did not go to Vietnam, but when his Army service obligation was up, he migrated to Canada and later competed in the 10,000 meters for Canada in the 1976 Olympics. Pat Hornbostel, another outstanding distance runner from OSU, went to Vietnam, survived his tour, but suffered a cruel injury, the loss of his lower legs to an explosive booby trap. Bill Rawson, who as a University of Missouri half-miler had many close 880-yard races against Perry, was offered a spot on the Quantico track team. He chose, however, to go to Vietnam. Second lieutenant Rawson, a platoon leader, was killed in June 1967, two months after he arrived in Vietnam.

My Introduction to Military Life

Gary Lower, who became the OU cross-country coach my senior year, was a colonel in the Oklahoma Army National Guard. Recognizing my uncertainty about the fork in my road ahead, he asked me to consider joining the Guard. I joined, became a private in the 45th Infantry, and in August 1969 took a Greyhound bus to Fort Polk, deep in the heart of Louisiana, to begin 18 weeks of basic and infantry training. This opportunity did not, however, clarify my running future. It was not certain that I would be able to train while at Fort Polk. Would an four-month hiatus mean that my pursuit of the sub-4 mile was finished?

On my first day of basic training, even before I was issued my uniforms, it became apparent that I was not in college anymore—that there would no longer be leisurely meals of T-bone steak and bowls of ice cream topped with peaches as there were in OU's dining hall for athletes. This point was driven home on my first trip through the chow line, where I encountered an officious specialist fourth-class who looked and spoke like the Soup Nazi, famous for his line, "no soup for you," in the Seinfeld television comedy series. His spatula control being less than perfect, the specialist dropped half of my serving of a meat product on the floor as he tried to place it on my tray. Sensing I had failed to stabilize the tray according to military standards, he let me know that *his* mess hall emphasized discipline and order more than cuisine, cajun or otherwise. "No more for you," he snapped with a harsh look, and he demoted me on the spot from dining room orderly (DRO! he would shout to get my attention) to the back sink, which involved a 16-hour daily shift of washing pots and pans in the traditional infantry mode, manually without rubber gloves.

With that introduction to chow-hall discipline, I feared it would be difficult to continue my runner training in the Army. I adjusted to military life quickly, however, and found ways to squeeze in workouts whenever we weren't on overnight field training. During the 18 weeks, I ran about one-third as much as I had been running, most of it in darkness, slower than normal, and untimed because I couldn't read my stopwatch in the dark. I ran what I would now call threshold interval workouts, which were relatively short and slow—at the anaerobic-threshold pace. I ran them on the one-fifth-mile oval not far from the post exchange. I ran longer distances occasionally on a weekend days.

The darkness concealed unusual hazards at Fort Polk. One night, when I jogged past three soldiers walking abreast, I was blindsided by one of them who was apparently disappointed with the quality of life the selective-service draft had presented him. He vented his anger about military life by slugging me in the face. I then did what any serious runner would have done. I advanced rapidly to the rear. They didn't try to catch me.

Lapping the Field in Combat Boots

I found unexpected delight in running the mile in combat boots. The mile was part of the physical training test, in which I was slow at the low crawl and fireman's carry, but untouchable in the run. No one in my company could stay within a lap of me on the five-laps-per-mile PT track. In the six times my company ran the PT test, I was timed in 4:40, 4:45, 4:49 twice, 5:00 and 5:06. The heavy boots made me less economical as a runner; they acted like speed governors, slowing my cadence with their rigid, elevated heels limiting the elastic energy storage and return of my biological springs.

When I lapped the field in the second PT test, the drill sergeant strode over to me as I crossed the finish line and shouted: "You're not finished, young man!" He apparently had not been paying close attention, but I convinced him, without incurring correctional pushups that I had indeed run the full distance. I later learned that Chris McCubbins had run 4:46 in his PT test at Fort Polk earlier in 1969 and that Chuck LaBenz, who ran 3:56 in the mile at Arizona State University, set the Army record of 4:23 in combat boots as a second lieutenant at Fort Benning, Ga., in 1972. I feel certain that no one questioned his lap counting.

Three weeks before I completed my training at Fort Polk, the Selective Service held a lottery, its first for the draft since World War II. The lottery number randomly selected for my birthday was 322. This number did not represent the lowest probability of being drafted (366 did), but it meant that I and every other eligible male born on the same date as I were unlikely to be among the 2.2 million men drafted for the war. The timing of the lottery did not matter to me, however, as I remained in the Guard and reserves for 10 years and went to Officer Candidate School, where the chief instructor of my class was Richard Rescorla, a fearsome tactical officer from Cornwall, England, who died a hero in the twin towers collapse in New York City on September 11, 2001. Like some of the track athletes who were drafted during the war, I was later given opportunities to apply my running ability to compete in international military competitions.

Returning to Civilian Life, Running Like A Deer

When I returned to Oklahoma in December 1969, I resumed my normal training, and six weeks later I raced again, this time in a 2-mile on a 10-lap-per-mile banked-board track in Oklahoma City. I surprised myself with a run-like-a-deer performance, finishing fourth in 8:56.4 with mile splits of 4:24 and 4:32. When I finished, one of the officials, a former coach at OU's arch-rival, OSU, approached me and yelled, "You're not finished!" It was a familiar and unwelcome accusation. Perhaps he believed I had not improved since he saw me race in Kansas City four years earlier. "Oh yes, I have finished," I told him. "I finished ahead of two OSU runners. Check with them."

Two weeks later I lowered my best time in the mile to 4:07.2 on the five-laps-per-mile board track in the Astrodome in Houston. With these two personal bests coming soon after my military stint at Fort Polk, I began to wonder whether I should cut back on training intensity, at least periodically to keep improving. I did cut back, but not because of what I learned in the military. I did because I began to see the effects of over-training. Unfortunately, I was not finished completely with 100-mile weeks.

Billy Mills' Long Hiatus Leading to Olympic Gold

I later learned that Billy Mills had an even more anomalous experience after a long break from training before the 1964 Olympics. It too involved military duty, and it led to a historic comeback. He was a three-time NCAA All-American in cross-country at the University of Kansas. When he graduated in 1962, his personal bests were 31 minutes in the 10K and 13:59 over a 3-mile cross-country course, performances that fell well short of making him a candidate for the U.S. Olympic team. Upon graduation, he entered the Marine Corps as a second lieutenant and gave up running.

* * *

"One belief I always had about distance running: You don't have to have a world of ability. If you work and put in the mileage, it shouldn't be hard to produce. But I didn't produce, not what I thought I should. So I was pretty well discouraged and disgusted. I felt I failed," he told Sport Magazine [11].

He did not train for a year and a half. In June 1963, at the urging of his wife, he ended his long break from running. He explained in the article: "I did a real easy half mile, and it wasn't difficult. As I ran more, I found myself a lot stronger than I had ever been. I was amazed."

Encouraged by the rapid return of his aerobic power, he began preparing to race in Marine Corps and inter-service track meets. At age 25, he won the inter-service 10,000 meters in 30:08, then just one year after he had resumed training, he placed second in the 10,000 at the U.S. Olympic Trials in a personal best of 29:10.4.

With his best performance 40 seconds slower than the top Olympic hopefuls in Tokyo, he was given no chance for a medal in a field that included two previous Olympic champions and the world record holder at 10,000 meters, Ron Clarke of Australia. But on a wet, cinder track in Tokyo in October 1964, he came up with what was surely a run-like-a-deer performance, winning in world-record time. He became the first American to win the Olympic 10,000. His victory was considered the number-one upset of the Tokyo Games. A year later, he broke the world record in the 6-mile with a 27:11.6, finishing in a tie with Gerry Lindgren in the AAU national championships.

How does one explain this unlikely improvement after a long layoff? What was the physiological basis for his minimal loss of power and rapid improvement after 1 ½ years away from training?

A long hiatus often means the end of a racing career. Subsequent comebacks are typically unsuccessful. Runners who don't stay active during the layoff don't get beyond the early stages of a comeback, thinking their bodies have undergone irreversible changes. The physiology of de-conditioning of runners has been the subject of several research studies. One apparent conclusion is that it is critical to remain consistently active. The longer the hiatus and the farther the runner departs from his or her best racing weight—the weight for which the biological springs of the legs are finely tuned—the less likely there will be a successful comeback.

It is apparent that the level of activity Mills maintained while not training to race prepared him for his remarkable success. Had it been bed rest or a couch-potato lifestyle, the ultimate outcome would have been vastly different. In his case, his layoff *was* active rest consisting of military activities in a Marine officer training course: marching, double-time, PT testing, field exercises, etc. Mills trained very hard at the University of Kansas; possibly he overtrained. In the period of active rest after leaving KU, his body probably overcompensated with the adaptations affecting aerobic and anaerobic power and running economy.

How Ryun's VO2max Changed After a Year Off

In his five-year physiological case study of Jim Ryun, Jack Daniels took measurements before and after Ryun took a year off following the 1968 Olympics[12]. During this year of inactivity, his maximal oxygen uptake dropped about 10 percent, and his VO2max (relative to his body weight, which increased by about 20 pounds), dropped about 20 percent, to 65.0 milliliters of oxygen per minute per kilogram of body weight. His highest VO2max of 81.0 was measured three years earlier, the year in which he set the world record of 3:51.1 in the mile. By 1972, two years after his hiatus, his maximal oxygen uptake had gradually returned to the same value as his 1967 measurement. At 165 pounds body weight, 5 pounds more than his 1967 weight, his VO2max was 78.3. He might have been ready to capture the gold medal in the '72 Olympics, but he was tripped and failed to finish in the quarterfinals.

When I attended the infantry officer basic course at Fort Benning, Georgia, in 1972, I became a friend and teammate of Greg Camp, an infantry officer who in 1968 set school records at West Point in the mile (4:05.8) and half mile (1:49) and achieved NCAA All-American status in the half mile. In 1969-70, he served a year in Viet Nam, and when he returned to Fort Benning, he resumed training and racing with the Atlanta Track Club. Within two years, he was consistently bettering his collegiate performances in the mile, improving to 4:03.0, and he was ready to improve even further.

In situations of total rest, some of the negative changes of deconditioning can occur rapidly. For example, in a 1986 study [13], when trained cyclists became sedentary for two months, their aerobic capacity dropped an average of 20 percent and heart stroke volume dropped 17 percent. Such changes can, however, be reversed, probably as rapidly as the loss occurs. I learned many years later that one of the greatest stars of American distance running, Bernard Lagat, had been routinely taking a five-week total break from running each year for several years. Lagat, a 3:47 miler, five-time Olympian, and two-time world champion, remained in top condition well into his 40s with the benefit of his yearly break. "Rest is a good thing,"he said.[14]

With the benefit of four months of lighter training at Fort Polk, I began my first unattached year of track with much-needed confidence boosters—personal bests in the mile and 2-mile. This lesson on training lighter, however, did not fully sink in. My training reverted to my original perception about how hard I should train and how often I should rest. I was unaware of the benefits of temporary de-conditioning with annual breaks such as Lagat's, and I did not have the confidence to experiment with this contrarian concept. I could not see that my training, racing, and resting were out of balance, and I could not easily throttle my zeal for training and racing. I never took off more than three days at a time until an injury years later forced me to do so.

Chapter Eight
Aerobic, Anaerobic and Arthur Lydiard

In February 1970, I traveled to Houston to run in the Astrodome, the eighth wonder of the world, as it was known when it opened five years earlier. There was some Texas-style hyperbole in that designation, but as the world's first indoor air-conditioned domed stadium, it was indeed a gawk-worthy wonder. My first visit came within a few days of Elvis Presley's first visit. He gave a press conference there in February leading up to his six concert performances, which would draw a total of 300,000 fans over three days. "It's a big place, man. It scares me," he said in the press conference.

The 1970 track meet drew about 30,000 fans over two days, which left 29,000 empty seats each session, making the crowd seem faraway and quiet—an ambience not likely to scare any of us runners. The Astrodome was indeed a big place, 18 stories tall, 9.5 acres under roof, and 42,200 cushioned seats which later increased to 67,000. A 352-yard banked-board track (five laps to the mile) was installed in 1969. It was larger, and faster, than all other indoor tracks in the U.S., which at that time were typically 10, 11, or 12 laps per mile banked or 8 laps unbanked. In sharp contrast, Pneumonia Downs, the indoor track that served OU athletes with Spartan adequacy from 1924 to 1986, was an eight-lap dirt track with sharp, steeply banked turns beneath the east side of the football stadium.

On the Astrodome's beautiful baby-blue track, I ran the mile, which had qualifying heats in the early afternoon and a final at 10 p.m. Both were tactical races with fast finishes. Favored was Marty Liquori of Villanova who had an exceptional kick that helped him make the '68 Olympic team at age 19 and to eventually run a 3:52.2 mile. The pace in the final was pedestrian for the first half, 2:08, before the field of nine unleashed a long dash to the finish. Liquori won by 1.1 seconds in 4:05.5, and I placed fifth in 4:07.2. My second-half split was 1:58.9, the fastest second half I had ever run in a mile race, but it wasn't enough to keep up with Liquori.

Conversation With the "Coach of Champions and Nobodies."

The next day I had a long conversation over lunch with an international coaching icon, Arthur Lydiard. He was known as a "coach of champions and nobodies" because he would coach anyone of any ability who sought his guidance on middle- or long-distance running. He did so in recognition that all runners have the potential to improve.

Three of the local athletes he trained in New Zealand starred in the 1960 Olympics in Rome. Peter Snell won the 800; Murray Halberg, the 5,000; and Barry Magee took the bronze in the marathon. Unlike some outstanding coaches, who recruited champions and made them greater, Lydiard took nobodies and made them champions by applying the training methods he developed by experimenting on himself for many years until he felt he had the perfect training program. At times he would run a marathon before breakfast, then another in the afternoon. Running seven days a week, he would cover up to 300 miles per week, but he found that running more than 100 a week made him feel stale.

He offered to coach me. At that time, I still felt like a nobody, and I politely declined his offer because I believed long-distance coaching was not practical for responsive feedback. There was no email, no texting; air mail was slow, and long-distance phone calls were expensive.

Having read much about him, I felt I knew all about his program, which involved three months of marathon training at 100 miles per week followed by two months of hill training, then three months of faster-paced low mileage workouts, referred to as speed work, during the track racing season. I told him I would be running his marathon training program in the fall.

He talked about training in terms of aerobic versus anaerobic running, and he was especially stern about limiting the anaerobic running. A handout he presented at a conference for coaches at the meet summarized his position on it with this paragraph.

***

"They use anaerobic running to excess. I always considered these (coaches) the menaces to the sport, as they continually overlook the problems associated with the use of excessive anaerobic training and are responsible for preventing the development of the potentially best of the sporting youth in their countries. Many look for quick methods with which to develop potential and invariably make use of disproportionate amounts of anaerobic running in comparison to the aerobic running."[15]

After my discussion with him, I felt I had a better understanding of the variations in pace and distance of his 100-mile-a-week regimen on only one workout a day. As it turned out, I did *not* have a full understanding, but I resolved to perform it in the fall exactly as he had written it.

Three Months of Lydiard's Marathon Training

I ran 13 weeks of his marathon training on the section roads and highways around Norman, Oklahoma, and did not stray from the prescribed workouts, either in distance or in level of effort, although his guidance on level of effort seemed vague. Relative to my previous 100-mile weeks on two workouts per day during the summers, there were major differences that affected my recovery. Included were runs 18 to 20 miles twice a week over hilly courses, faster paced 10 mile runs twice a week on flat courses, and there were no rest days; I had always had one rest day per week. All the workouts were to be run at what he described at "near best aerobic effort". I knew this included those listed at one-quarter and one-half effort, but I wasn't sure about the three-quarter effort 10-mile on Tuesdays, which I assumed were to be run at the lactate threshold, one of which I ran 53:30. Here is what I ran:

> Monday: 18 miles at one-quarter effort on a moderately flat course at a pace ranging from 6:40 to 7:10 per mile.
> Tuesday: 10 miles at three-quarter effort on a flat course at a pace of 5:20 to 5:50 per mile.
> Wednesday: 20 miles at one-quarter effort on a reasonably flat course at 6:40 to 7:00 per mile.

Thursday: 16 miles at one-quarter effort on a reasonably flat course at 6:40 to 7:05 per mile.

Friday: 10 miles at one-half effort on an undulating course at 5:45 to 6:10 per mile.

Saturday: 14 miles at one-quarter effort on any type terrain at 7:00 to 7:10 per mile.

Sunday: 12 miles of fartlek on the OU golf course averaging 6:30 to 6:50 per mile.

Many years later, when I read *Running with Lydiard*, his book published in 2000, it seemed that he was no longer firm about 100 miles a week. In describing how he developed his program, he wrote that he tried running as little as 50 miles a week and as much as 300 a week at near his best aerobic pace before he decided on 100. Surprisingly, however, he added that supplemental running at a slower pace at other times in the day was beneficial—once he learned that this helped his recovery and rate of improvement. He wrote, "Running is, without question, the best exercise for runners and, as long as we watch the degree of effort, we cannot really do too much."[16]

I believe Lydiard was conditionally correct, but his stated condition, to watch the degree of effort, was impractical. On a hilly course, for example, a runner will engage the fast-twitch muscles to run anaerobically uphill and downhill. All mileage is not equal, and all runners' responses are not equal.

How Peter Snell Developed Under Lydiard

I later learned that Lydiard's greatest star, Peter Snell, had difficulty running 100 miles per week, particularly with the longest run, a challenging 22-miler called the Waiatarua on the steep foothills in the Waitakere Ranges in New Zealand.

Snell had a strong background in sports; in his youth, he participated in tennis, cricket, cross-country, and track. In track, he ran the 880 and the mile. At age 19, he ran 1:59.5 in the 880, and at 20, just before he began training with Lydiard, 1:52.8. Once under Lydiard's tutelage, he apparently improved rapidly in his aerobic capacity, but just a few months before the 1960 Olympic team selection, he developed a stress fracture of the tibia that required two to three months of total inactivity. The injury threatened to knock him out of contention for the Olympic team, but his fitness returned quickly enough to run 1:49.2 in the Auckland Championships to clinch a spot on the team. He won the gold medal in the 800 in 1:46.48, an Olympic record. In preparing for the 1962 racing season, differences arose over his approach to speed training, and Lydiard withdrew as his coach two years before the Tokyo Olympics, in which Snell won the 800 in 1:45.1. and the 1500 in 3:38.1. [17]

Bowerman's Opinion of 100 Miles Per Week

When Bill Bowerman took Oregon's world record 4x1-mile team to tour New Zealand in 1962, he met Lydiard, learned about his training methods, and tried jogging with his group. In the fall of 1963, Bowerman's runners tried the marathon training program Lydiard advocated. According to author Chris Walsh in his book, *The Bowerman System*, most of the runners became so fatigued with the schedule, they had to stop training after one week. Though Bowerman had great respect for Lydiard, he did not agree with the high mileage. "There is no better distance coach in the world (than Lydiard)," said Bowerman, who rejected this aspect of the program. "I've coached a dozen (actually 16 in total) sub-4:00 milers and I've never seen any of them who didn't run into trouble training over 80 miles a week."

Bowerman was impressed with the jogging program Lydiard established in New Zealand, and he later co-authored with Dr. Richard Harris the book *Jogging* which was published in 1967. The book's introduction acknowledged Lydiard's great impact: "In New Zealand, thanks to the work of Arthur Lydiard, the New Zealand Olympic coach, jogging is almost a way of life. The active citizenry took to it in a big way." The book sold over a million copies in six different languages.[18]

Having run Lydiard's marathon training, exactly as prescribed in the fall of 1970, I agreed with Bowerman, although I did not read his assessment until years later. I believe it needed instructions for tailoring to accommodate anyone who recovers and adapts less quickly than others. Perhaps something as simple as the subjective controls Bowerman applied at Oregon—to always finish a workout feeling exhilarated and to under-train rather than over-train. Lydiard's program is based on "best aerobic pace", but I drifted over the anaerobic threshold on at least one long run per week. Perhaps Snell did also each time he ran the hilly 22-mile Waiatarua.

I had high expectations for what the 13 weeks of training would do for me. I did not judge the results until the following spring, and I ran fairly well in that track season of 1971. I did not however, see as much improvement as in previous track seasons. Perhaps it was because I was reaching my maximum—the peak or plateau—of my aerobic capacity, my VO2max, which all runners eventually reach. Or perhaps the standard indicators of overtraining—sore muscles, poor sleep, elevated morning heart rate, low energy, and mood changes—are not sensitive enough to alert a runner that the point of optimal intensity of training has been passed, that more recovery time is needed. routinely.

I believe I could have learned much more and gotten greater benefit from Lydiard's program had he coached me in person.

Chapter Nine
Cunningham, Ryun and the Steamroller

I received a telegram in April 1971 while still at OU, finishing my engineering courses. In that pre-internet era, the telegram was a medium for conveying either good news or bad news. It was a little too expensive for anything in between. This one, which came via my coach, J.D. Martin, was of the good-news variety. It was an invitation from Kansas coach Bob Timmons to compete in the Glenn Cunningham mile at the Kansas Relays four days later.

I competed in the Cunningham Mile the previous year, but without a telegram invitation and without distinction. The Kansas Relays had long been the grand stage for America's best milers—Glenn Cunningham, Wes Santee, and Jim Ryun—so this telegram was scrapbook-worthy. It even had my name spelled correctly (Blewett, not Blewitt as president Joseph Biden's Irish grandmother spelled her name, nor Bluett, Bluet, Blueit, or Bluitt, which are variations of our surname). Glenn Cunningham's name also made it special, even though his first name was spelled incorrectly, leaving the second "n" off Glenn, probably the result of a mistake on a telegrapher's keystroke.

Glenn Cunningham was an icon of track and field in the 1930s, a true hero of the mile of the same stature of Jim Ryun and Roger Bannister. "He was to indoor track what Babe Ruth was to baseball," wrote Fred Wilt. When he was 7 years old, his legs were so badly burned in a rural Kansas schoolhouse fire, the family doctor suggested amputation. Two years passed before he was able to walk again. Eventually he began running to strengthen his legs. With remarkable resilience he became the fastest high-school miler in the U.S. He lowered the national scholastic mile record to 4:24.7 in May 1930.

At the University of Kansas, he improved rapidly and became the world's best miler, setting world records of 4:06.7 outdoors and 4:04.4 indoors. At 5-foot-9 and 154 pounds, he possessed the natural speed of a sprinter that helped him dominate over a wide range of distances. He set world records at 600 yards and 1,000 yards indoors and 800 meters outdoors (1:49.7). His best time for 440 yards was 47.2 seconds (equivalent to 46.9 for 400 meters). Reporters called him "the Iron Man of Kansas."

Though the telegram did not mention that Jim Ryun would be running, I knew that he probably would be and that this would be his last Cunningham Mile appearance. He was then a year away from his ill-fated return to the Olympic Games. For me, it meant one final opportunity to engage in a hopeless chase of the Kansas star or to be towed to a personal best in his wake. This would be my last race in the Kansas Relays, the sixth of six unimpressive races between 1966 and 1971. In three of those, I ran behind Ryun, trailing by large margins, twice in the Cunningham Mile and once on the mile anchor leg of the distance medley relay.

Chewing Gum on The Run

That relay in 1969 revealed that I lacked the ability to run and chew gum at the same time. Dennis Cotner, OU's star intermediate hurdler, advised me that chewing gum would keep my mouth from drying out from nervousness during the race. His advice made that ordinary race memorable for me, even though our team placed fourth, behind the Kansas foursome. Anchored by Ryun, the Jayhawk team broke the world record.

Soon after I took the baton, I knew the gum was overmatched. It went dry at the same rapid rate as my salivary glands and became a flexible superglue, firmly attaching my tongue to the roof of my mouth with holding power equivalent to sidewalk spearmint on a shoe bottom. I was unprepared for the difficulty of removing it at mid-race, and trying to do so while holding a baton affected both my mechanics and my concentration, costing me a couple of seconds for sure. Chewing gum, I learned years later has circulatory benefits for one's brain because of the presence of tiny one-way valves in the facial veins at the lower jaw (more on venous valves in Chapter 20). Studies have found that gum chewing is associated with heightened alertness, quicker reaction times, improved sustained attention. None of these, however, offset the adhesive effect on my tongue.

My fortunes were better in the 1971 Cunningham Mile in which I improved my personal best to 4:04.5. I ran even splits of 61 seconds for each quarter and felt good, but I should have kicked the last quarter in 58 or 59 seconds. The pack began pulling away just before the start of the bell lap, and psychologically I felt like a loose caboose. I did not run like a deer and I began to feel the full weight of The Bear in the last lap. I placed eighth out of nine runners. Ryun ran about a 54-second last quarter to win in 3:55.8. Von Ruden took second in 3:57.2.

A Strange, Mostly Successful Battle Against Mud

To me, the most exciting Glenn Cunningham Mile was the one I watched, sitting in the stands not far from Glenn Cunningham himself in my freshman year. It was a thrilling, crowd-pleasing race that followed a strange prelude to the Saturday afternoon session. That morning, I anchored the OU freshman 4-mile relay, one of several races moved to the Haskell Institute track because of the rain. This was the cinder track on which Billy Mills trained and raced before transferring to the University of Kansas. There, on a very soft, wet track, I won my first collegiate medal (bronze) by out-leaning another rising star from Haskell Institute, Roy Oldperson.

Ryun, then a freshman with a personal best of 3:55.3, was expected to thrill thousands of his ardent fans by producing the first sub-4-minute mile in the 41 years the Kansas Relays had been held.

There was, however, a problem. It had been raining almost continuously for three days, so without divine intervention or novel mud-drying technology, the cinder track was likely to soon resemble any old muddy farm road in Kansas. Not to let this opportunity slip away in the mire, the University hired a steamroller, a double-drum 10-ton monster, to groom the track.

I found a seat in the stadium early and watched the steamroller crawl around the oval many more times than seemed necessary to squeeze the water out of the running surface. I assumed it would complete its assignment before the first of many races would begin. Surprisingly, however, it did not stop when the races began. Of course, I had to remind myself that this track-grooming was for the benefit of the world's greatest miler, Kansas' favorite son, Jim Ryun. The steamroller had priority access until the Glenn Cunningham Mile went to the starting line, so it persisted in its urgent mission.

The driver steered with his shoulder turned toward the infield to ensure a clear view, front and rear as he maintained an in-and-out weaving pattern. As runners approached, he steered to the outer lanes, and as they passed, he returned to the inner lanes. Safety prevailed, luckily. Fears of runners being being accidentally compacted into the mud were unfounded. It was a remarkable display of runner-and-vehicle synchronicity, surely one unique in the history of track and field.

Each year, Glenn Cunningham would drive 140 miles to KU from his home in the small town of Leon, and from the stands would watch the race named in his honor. On this day, I sat about five meters away from the icon himself. Glenn Jr. was also a spectator after winning the high school mile race the previous day, spattered with mud in 4:22.1. Glenn Jr. would eventually don a Kansas uniform and compete in the race named for his father. He would run well, his mechanics and performance very much like his father's. His best mile time as a collegian was about the same as his father's indoor world-record time three decades earlier.

The steamroller found a parking spot just before the milers stepped onto the track. Despite its hours of work, the running surface was less than perfect, but its softness seemed somehow to affect everyone except Ryun. In the Relays' Thursday session, Ryun had run a 3:59.0 mile with a 53.6 last lap in the freshman distance medley relay. In the featured race Saturday, however, there were no apparent effects of fatigue or imperfect footing, as he delighted the crowd with a new collegiate record of 3:55.8. The second-place finisher was John Camien, who had won the bronze medal in the previous World Championships. He finished 60 yards behind Ryun in 4:04.8. The next morning, newspapers across the U.S. reported on the freshman's stellar performance. The Associated press story of April 24, 1966 read:

> "Jim Ryun, the amazing 18-year-old Kansas freshman, ran
> a 3:55.8 in the Glenn Cunningham Mile at the 41st
> Kansas Relays Saturday, just one-half second off his own
> American Record and the best time in the world this year.
> Ryun, 6-2, 160 pounds, sprinted the last quarter in 55.1
> seconds and just missed the American record he set last
> June in the National AAU. Teammate Tom Yergovich led

Ryun after the first lap, but Ryun spurted ahead just before the end of the first one-half mile and widened his gap over John Camien, the former Emporia State star, the rest of the way. Ryun's quarter times were 57.6, 61.1, 62.0, and 55.1 as he hit the three quarters in 3:00.7."[19]

Wes Santee's Assessment of Jim Ryun

In an adjacent column was another Associated Press story bearing the headline, "Wes Santee Rates Ryun Perfect Runner." Just 300 words long, it attempted to address the questions that followed Ryun wherever he went: How can a runner so young achieve such superiority? What makes this miler different from the rest? Santee, who 12 years earlier set the Cunningham Mile record that Ryun smashed by over 7 seconds, was quoted:

"If the perfect distance runner could be created from the ground up, he would come out looking very much like Jim Ryun. Ryun is the proper height and weight, has speed, plenty of desire, and the most powerful-looking pair of thighs I've ever seen on a distance runner. That's where he gets his strength."[20]

Santee, I believe, was partially correct about Ryun's source of strength. It is interesting to read, however, the speculation based only on physical characteristics before scientific instruments and techniques became available for research into the anatomy and physiology of speed and endurance in the 1950s and 60s. When Jesse Owens was breaking records as a sprinter in the mid-1930s, the conjecture included comments about pliable muscles; muscles that were tapering and seldom bunched; fine legs that would inspire any sculptor; and cell structure of the nervous system capable of carrying strong stimulus. These, of course, seem humorous and irrelevant for producing great speed or endurance.

In the middle of the twentieth century, however, even physicians seemed clueless. Fred Wilt noted that in the early 1950s some physicians stated that there was nothing unusual or abnormal about the physiological makeup of Emil Zatopek, then the world's greatest distance runner. [21] They obviously couldn't measure the performance of Zatopek's powerful heart in action.

***
Jack Daniels' Five-Year Study of Ryun

A year after Ryun's debut in the Cunningham Mile, Jack Daniels, a PhD physiologist, coach, and two-time Olympian, began a series of nine tests and measurements on Ryun over a five-year period in search of the secret to his phenomenal ability. He published his findings in a journal article entitled: "Running with Jim Ryun: A Five-Year Study." [21] The testing showed that at age 20, Ryun could produce a very high level of aerobic power, which in terms of maximal oxygen uptake was 81.0 milliliters of oxygen per minute per kilogram of body weight. Daniels noted, however, that this was no higher than that measured for Don Lash, who in 1936 set a world record of 8:58.4 in the two-mile.[23] Lash's 2-mile was 33 seconds slower than Ryun's American record of 8:25.2, and his best mile was 16 seconds slower than Ryun's 1967 world record of 3:51.1.

Daniels ran other tests and found that what differentiated Ryun from other elite runners was his exceptional running economy, meaning that he applied less power than other elite runners in running at various speeds. Running economy is affected by many factors, but the most important one may be the ability to recycle energy and amplify power with the biological springs of the legs. It is still mysterious, like the phenomenon of running like a deer.

Ryun's record in the Cunningham Mile still stands as of 2022. In the eighty-second Kansas Relays in 2009, it withstood a challenge from Alan Webb, the runner who in 2001 broke Ryun's national high school record in the mile with a 3:53.43. Running in a light rain on KU's all-weather track in front of a sparse crowd, Webb won the Cunningham Mile in 3:58.90. Ryun was at the starting line. At age 63, he was the honorary starter.

Chapter Ten
Psyching up, not out

In the 1960s, newspaper sports sections devoted lots of space to track and field. My recent viewing of an old sports column clipped from *The Oklahoma Journal*, a state-wide newspaper that was published from 1964 to 1980, reminded me of those days. The column was written by *Journal* sports editor, Doug Ford, on what must have been a slow-news day in 1966.

Apparently, he was inspired to write it upon receiving a press release from the OU Sports Information Office. The release mentioned my encounter with a skunk while I ran one morning before dawn, an encounter described in Chapter 19. Mr. Ford had never written a sports column about a skunk, I assume, so he saw a way to increase the variety and humor of his columns, and to practice the art of hyperbole.

My parents in Lawton did not subscribe to *The Journal*, but Mr. Ford's column convinced them never to do so. They were appalled at what he wrote. I thought it was embarrassing and somewhat odiferous, not because of the skunk's role but because it emphasized that I had been an outstanding loser. There was some truth to that, I admit, but I disagreed that I had been one of the best losers in the business. That's hyperbole. I did not, however, lose any sleep over it. I had given him quite a lot of loser insight when he interviewed me. I was so new to being written about that I had not yet learned the difference between good press and bad press in sports. The column began like this.

> "Two years ago when he first began running the distances at Oklahoma, few people had heard of Bill Blewett and

most of them have forgotten since. Still, he thinks big. Dancing in his head are visions of becoming an "international-class runner." In case you don't know what that is, Jim Ryun is one. It's a mighty long way from winning the Boomer Conference 880-yard run, which is one of the few races Blewett hasn't lost. For years, Bill Blewett has been a loser, one of the best in the business. He finished so far behind everyone else he had to read the paper the next morning to find out who was in the race. His strategy for distance running was painfully simple and equally successful: he would study each opponent at the starting line, conclude that he doubtlessly would lose, and he did just that. All that is history now. Early one morning last fall, getting in his daily six miles in near-darkness, Bill spooked a skunk and found that running was not intended to be a slow process. He began to work up a whole new idea of himself."

The hyperbole continues throughout the column, but anyone who read the whole piece would have seen that it was really about rising from an unlikely beginning to become OU's best distance runner as a sophomore through the recognition that in foot racing, psychology matters.

Applying Positive Visualization

In reading the book *Psycho-Cybernetics*, a best-seller in the '60s, my approach to racing went from psyching *out* to psyching *up*. The book's mental exercise I remember best was practicing basketball shots mentally, visualizing the ball, the basket,, and the shots, mostly the successful ones.

In applying this visualization to racing, the important change was to control my thoughts in the half hour before I would go to the starting line. In my first two years of racing, my habit in warming up for a race was to dwell on the pain I would have to endure. I would worry about how my legs were feeling, about what would happen when I tromped on the gas pedal to move up in the pack or start a kick. Would my engines sputter? If my mind dwelled on my pain and being unable to keep up with the leaders, that would become the reality.

After reading the book, I began to focus my thoughts on the races in which I ran like a deer, which, midway through my sophomore year at OU were still few in number. I had not yet run my personal best in the indoor meet at the University of Wisconsin. I had not yet run against Jim Ryun in our dual meet in Norman, and I had not yet raced 4 miles against Wichita State's Roy Oldperson, the outstanding Native American runner and NAIA All-American at Haskell Institute.

The 4-mile race against Roy came in the following cross-country season. It took place in Wichita on a gently rolling golf course that featured greens made of sand, not grass. I viewed Roy as superior, but having read *Psycho-Cybernetics*, I resolved to maintain close contact with him in the race. I ran right beside him, almost touching elbows for the full distance. I simply focused on maintaining that minimal separation between us. I told myself I was going to win, and I did not let him gain an inch on me. We reached the mile marks in 4:42, 9:50, and 14:50 before I sprinted ahead in the final 100 meters to win by 2 seconds in 19:53. As a bonus, my time bettered the course record of 19:54 held by another fine Kansas runner, John Mason, who ran a 3:43.04 1500 meters and 8:48.24 steeplechase for Fort Hayes State. My teammate Carey Hollis, a freshman who had run 4:09.9 and 9:11.0 in high school in Hobbs, N.M., finished third, 46 seconds behind me in third place.

Racing with confidence builds confidence, I learned. The Wichita race was a real confidence booster, another positive performance to think about during the warmup of future races.

I am not trying to assert that positive visualization is all-powerful. It is not, but it is an important ingredient of success in racing. Races are battles against pain, but pain has multiple forms that vary with the distance of the race. You can chose the parameters of pain to make pain a weapon you control, to make it your ally, if you have the ability and the confidence to do so. Consider this classic example.

Bob Day's Courageous Race

In the spring of 1965, Bob Day, a 20-year-old sophomore at UCLA, set the NCAA record of 3:56.4 in the mile, a mark that was broken a year later by Ryun at the Kansas Relays. A week before the 1966 NCAA Championships in Berkeley, Calif., Day recognized that he had very little chance of beating the defending champion, Morgan Groth of Oregon State. Though he was in peak shape, having set the NCAA record just one week earlier, he knew that Groth had the advantage because of his great finishing speed.

Groth, an Olympian, was the American record holder in the 880-yard run (1:47.5). In the qualifying round two days before the final, he and Day had finished dead even at 4:03.7 . Day knew his only hope of winning was to push the pace faster than ever before, to build an insurmountable lead. Not only did he have to prepare mentally for Groth's speed, he had to summon his courage and confidence for a battle with The Bear.

Day put his strategy into action, running 55.3 seconds for the first 440-yard lap and 1:53.4 for the first 880, which at the time was probably the fastest first half ever run in a mile race. He held his quick pace through the ¾-mile mark in 2:54.7, at which point Groth and 10 other competitors appeared to be in a separate race of their own. But The Bear caught up with Day on the backstretch of the fourth lap and climbed aboard. It was a big bear, an Ursa Major, which slowed him to a 34.6-second final 220 yards. By the time he reached the homestretch, he was beset by a condition described by another Latin phrase, *rigor mortis*, meaning stiffness of death. His last 50 yards was so slow that he seemed barely able to move at all. Suddenly, there was doubt about his ability to even finish the race. Two runners charged down the home stretch to close the lead to just 5 yards. Day summoned the power to hold off their late charge, however, to become the NCAA champion in 4:01.8. Groth finished a soundly beaten fifth in 4:04.7.

Sports writers described the race as an unforgettable classic. Day described it as the most painful race of his career, one seared into his memory. He probably knew The Bear would find him on the last lap, that the lactate concentration in his blood was climbing steadily, but he did not know what he would reach first, his breaking point or the finish line. His strategy forced the other runners to carry The Bear if they tried to stay close or to give up the chase if they didn't.

In the interest of truthful disclosure, my race against Jim Ryun in the 1967 dual meet against Kansas was nothing like Bob Day's race against Morgan Groth. Jim Ryun did not run according to plan in that race, nor did I. There was no championship at stake, no element of courage, no battle with Ursa Major in that race. I did not know what the heck was going on. Kansas coach Bob Timmons didn't inform me that the Kansas strategy was to take it easy and not worry about the finishing time. And I was afraid to look back as the sound of footsteps drew closer. As Satchel Paige once said, "don't look back. Something might be gaining on you."

Longer Races: Slower Accumulation, Longer Pain Tolerance

There are other ways, I learned, to deal with pain successfully. Run on your rival's shoulder and let your lactate build slowly. Avoid full-blown rigor mortis.

The slow buildup also works on long-distance races but with a caveat: On uphills and downhills or in response to surges, don't let your lactate level rise too high too far from the finish. It will come down unless the rival ahead of you has the resolve of Bob Day.

The late stage of a marathon may be the toughest situation. There, one faces the problem of glycogen depletion and the resulting loss of power as the muscles switch to fat as a fuel or lose power due to dehydration. There is also the pain of muscle damage, heralded perhaps by a limp that gradually worsens. There too is the side stitch, caused by a loss of power from the respiratory muscles due to dehydration or glycogen depletion. Here is a solution to a constellation of pain such as this, though it is one seldom applied: quit the race or at least slow down, unless it is a race of ultimate importance. Accept defeat without guilt and save yourself for another day.

I learned from Bob Day's experience and gradually built the confidence to try what he did. It proved to be a winning approach in many of my races, such as my two personal-best indoor 2-miles in 1975, in my personal-best mile in 1972, and in the Stone Mountain 10-mile in Georgia in 1972 when I matched strides with Furman University star Lee Fidler for the full distance. In each race my thoughts were not on pain but on the essence of the Runner's Creed: *I will win. If I cannot win, I will run faster than ever before.*

Chapter Eleven
Well-aimed poison arrows

As any good mythologist knows, Thetis, the mother of Achilles, bears some responsibility for the injury in 1968 that caused a major setback in my quest to run a sub-4 mile.

Seeking to make her son immortal, Thetis dipped Achilles into the River Styx as an infant. According to legend, wherever the magical water touched his body, he became invincible. Unfortunately, Thetis did not change her grip and double dip, so the heel by which she held him remained dry and forever vulnerable.

Achilles grew up to become a great warrior. He was invincible in battle until Apollo, who was aware of the heel vulnerability, conspired with a Trojan prince named Paris to shoot a poison arrow into Achilles' heel. Hitting a fast-moving heel is a shot every archer knows to be extremely difficult, but Apollo guided the arrow to its target. Achilles became a battlefield fatality and was immortalized by the location of his wound. In reverence to this great mythological warrior, word processing software in the modern era automatically capitalizes the word Achilles as the common name for the heel cord, which is formally known as the calcaneal tendon.

That's the mythological explanation, which may evoke skepticism, but the story illustrates that Achilles tendon injuries have probably been affecting runners for thousands of years. For those who do battle on the tracks and fields of friendly strife, Achilles tendons are to this day a major point of weakness for even the strongest athletes. An estimated 52 percent of distance runners will suffer injury to their Achilles tendons in their careers.[24] As one who has suffered the wound of Achilles, I have learned, as many others have, that such an injury can diminish—or finish—a running career.

The Non-Mythological Explanation

Now for the scientific explanation. The Achilles tendon, though beautifully designed for utility in various modes — running, walking, jumping, and standing on two feet—has a materials problem. The tendons consist of bundles of collagen fibrils that under an electron microscope look like long, thin, coiled springs. These fibrils are susceptible to injury because they are not actually elastic, as is a coiled steel spring. As the best available spring material in the anatomical inventory, the fibrils are merely viscoelastic. This means that they can stretch only so far before the fibrils in the tendon's rope-like structure begin to deform or break.

When the fibrils become over-stressed quickly, stretching more than about 5 percent of their length, they can deform or break, resulting in poison-arrow-like pain. Here is another design problem. The pain that warns the runner that damage has occurred is often delayed by at least a day. So without immediate pain, the runner can increase the damage in a race or a workout of multiple repetitions only to learn the following day that substantial damage has occurred.

Running is a series of leaps. With natural foot mechanics, most of the stress of descending from each leap, about 2.7 times body weight for example, is magnified by leverage to produce force equal to about 7 times body weight on the Achilles tendon. With a cross-section area of about 0.15 square inch, this means that the tendon of a 155-pound runner becomes stressed to about 8,000 pounds per square inch with each stride.[25] This is about half the stress needed to break a healthy tendon; however, rapid acceleration or simply a faster pace can increase the stress. The accumulation of minor injury, the tearing of a few fibrils, can make the tendon more likely to break. Collagen fibrils can also be weakened by drugs, such as certain antibiotics, making a runner more susceptible. It is also more vulnerable in muscle fatigue resulting from glycogen depletion or lactate accumulation.

If collagen fibers were designed for rapid repair as are muscle fibers —with satellite cells in reserve within each muscle fiber waiting to be called to action, and with abundant capillary support—injuries to the tendon would be less serious. Ceasing to run long enough for healing to occur is the answer, but to most distance runners, taking time off is anathema. Achilles tendon injuries almost always worsen and persist longer than muscle injuries.

I did not know all this about the Achilles tendon in the summer of 1968 when I decided to run an interval workout of 40 x 220 yards with a 220 jog for rest three times per week. On the recovery day following each interval day, I ran 17 miles. Even though I ran it at a slower, steady pace, it was much too far to be a recovery workout. Running the 220s in long spikes on a hard cinder track resulted in the heel dropping lower than the toe (a negative foot angle) when the calf muscles fatigued. This seemed to produce greater stress on the muscle-tendon juncture. That summer thus became the season of pain because I ignored the soreness from Paris' poison arrow. It became chronic, with pain rising, falling, and persisting incredibly for the next 19 years.

The Division of Labor in the Legs

There is a division of labor in runners' legs: The upper legs and hips produce the power, and the lower legs and feet amplify the power. This may seem like an over-simplification, but it has been well demonstrated by South African runner Oscar Pistorious, who raced on J-shaped springs in place of his lower legs, which had been amputated just below the knee. This 2012 Olympian achieved a best time in the 400-meter dash of 45.07 seconds, running on springs of optimal elastic stiffness, perfectly adjusted in tension to his body weight. The J-shaped springs return close to 100 percent of the kinetic energy stored and released in the runner's vertical oscillations and horizontal braking. At best, the biological springs of the normal human legs return about half, and much less than that when the calf muscles become fatigued in a race or become inadequate in strength when a runner gains weight without an attendant gain in the strength of calf muscles and tendons.

Saving just half of the kinetic energy of up and down and braking is huge, as it saves a large portion of the energy cost of running. This potential can be seen in comparing the performance of speed-skaters versus runners. The 1500-meter world record for speed skating is 1:40.17. For running, it is 3:26.0. The skater takes less than half as long to cover 1500 meters, because of the greater energy efficiency that can be achieved on the ice without having to launch and land repeatedly in a series of leaps.

A few years after my last race, when I was in my late 40s and 25 pounds heavier than my best racing weight, I lost my natural foot mechanics. I became a heel striker, which seemed an appropriate downgrade, since by then I had ended my racing career and had become a fitness runner. Consequently, I had to rely on the elevated shoe heel to absorb the road shock. Doing so became even more important as I aged and began to lose the fat pads of my feet. My Achilles tendons became irrelevant for shock absorbing, power amplifying, and energy recycling.

Advent of the Elevated Heel

Cushioning shoe heels are popular among fitness runners. Such heels may suffice as shock absorbers in long slow distance runs before one develops adequate strength and endurance of the lower leg muscles. Despite my sincere efforts, which included losing about 15 pounds, it took me years to get off my heels as a jogger and to approach—but not fully achieve—natural foot mechanics after I lost them. I could keep the heel up at a speed of about 9 minutes per mile. But because the ground-strike force of the leaps increases with speed, I could not do so at a faster pace.

Running in shoes with elevated heels, if done to excess, can cause the calf muscles to gradually weaken. Shoe heels have two original purposes: to make the wearer look taller and to prevent the feet from slipping out of the stirrups when riding a horse. For short actors in western movies, like 5-foot-6 Alan Ladd, heels served both purposes.

There were no elevated heels on running shoes when I began to train as a runner in 1965. I had good, natural foot mechanics in my Adidas flats, which had no elevation at the heels. Heels came along about 1972 when Bill Bowerman, a co-founder of Nike, developed a shoe for Kenny Moore, who had injured himself wearing the thin-soled Tiger Bangkok racing shoes on a long run. As the story goes, Bowerman decided to make the heel thickness equal to that of a normal street shoe so that it would feel natural. The shoe became the Nike Cortez, and elevated heels became a permanent feature on running shoes.[26]

The advent of the heel benefitted fitness joggers but not racers, particularly young runners hoping to develop into champions. With the ideal foot-strike angle and thin heels (zero to 4 mm drop), there should be less than an inch between the heel and the ground. In wearing a typical running shoe with a thick heel, the heel of the shoe fills this space, and more readily comes in contact with the ground unless the runners increase their foot-strike angle. Running with an increased foot-strike angle, however, hastens fatigue. In running long distance in elevated heels, the calf muscles can gradually become superfluous and weaken, causing the runner to rely on the heel of the shoe for shock absorption. Fatigue of the calf muscles in longer runs can hasten this maladaptation to heel-striking.

Though heel-striking may seem perfectly comfortable and natural, it frequently leads to shin splints and stress fractures. Reversing this change is not easy. It requires building strength and endurance in the lower-leg muscles and relearning the coordination of natural foot mechanics.

Healthy Achilles tendons are absolutely essential to a runner's speed and endurance. They are the industrial-strength biological springs that recycle energy, amplify power, and absorb road shock. When one or both of the tendons become damaged, causing pain and reducing elastic stiffness, running performances can suffer greatly.

Knowing all this helped me understand why I injured my Achilles, why the soreness persisted for years, why I should have been very protective of my Achilles tendons, and why I ceased to improve in the mile. The persistent Achilles soreness, however, was just part of the reason I could not frequently summon the phenomenon of running like a deer.

Chapter Twelve
Imperfect workouts

I learned about suicide sprints in my brief and unremarkable high school football season of 1964. Also known as killer dillers, this type of workout is a go-to for coaches who believe in the aphorism, *no pain no gain*. Intended to build endurance, these workouts usually involve sprinting the length or width of the playing field, so the sprints are typically no longer than 100 yards. They are made challenging by keeping the rest interval very short, usually the time it takes to turn around, inhale deeply, and go again. The pain comes from rapid lactate build-up, which quickly results in being unable to sustain proper mechanics and speed. This makes the workout a stimulus for poor, inefficient mechanics. Injuries can follow, and sometimes in the heat of summer, death can stalk the poorly conditioned, dehydrated athlete.

I imagine some coaches might quote Friedrich Nietzsche as they oversee a workout of suicide sprints: "What does not kill me makes me stronger." Applied to sports physiology, that's nonsense.

In running sports, extreme workouts have greater variety, but can be more brutal in their duration and intensity in the misconception that punishing a runner to the margins of abuse can build confidence and improve conditioning. Some coaches love them, even though they are about as effective at building endurance as a cat-of-nine-tails.

The main goal of runner training is adaptation—changes to the body's structure and function for greater endurance and greater speed afoot. Most adaptations are completed incrementally *after* the bout of exercise ends. Consequently, every workout has two phases—the exercise phase and the recovery phase. If recovery—repairing muscle and other tissues, restoring glycogen, and rehydrating—is not complete before the next workout begins, the workout is incomplete. A deficit of recovery can begin and grow into declining performance or injury.

An incomplete workout is an imperfect workout. Imperfect workouts are particularly bad for perfectionists like myself because we strive to complete them as prescribed, and we ignore the body's signals that urge us to slow down or stop. We also let mileage goals interfere with the recovery phase of the workout.

My Most Memorable Imperfect Workouts

In my youth, I believed that extremely hard workouts somehow had positive effects on speed and endurance. I endured a few tough ones, and I can say that none of them brought improvement in my race performances in the days or weeks afterwards. Here are some of my most memorable imperfect workouts.

18 x 880 in 2:20 to 2:22 with a 2-minute rest after each. A new assistant coach my senior year at OU prescribed this workout for me because he felt I was in a slump. He believed that the remedy for most slumps is to work harder, a common misconception in running sports. I was resistant to this workout, but I did it. The coach had the final word. Once I started it, my perfectionism kicked in. The result: I completed it but developed soreness in my lower back and hip that stayed with me for a month, and I ran poorly in races during that period.

88 x 100. This workout, a longer but more gentle variant of suicide sprints (moderate pace, more rest, less lactate) was prescribed for a group of us runners by a visiting track alumnus, who felt it was a good pep-me-up workout. We ran it on the grass. We had leaden legs afterwards but thankfully, no injuries resulted.

122 repetitions of 150s, 100s, 220s, and 260s. These 122 reps were the total between two workouts, morning and evening, on a summer day in 1970 in Santa Monica, California. They were under the direction of Mihali Igloi, the famous, demanding Hungarian coach whose runners collectively set 23 world records before he defected to the U.S. in 1956. I ran the workouts with a small group on the grass median strip of San Vicente Boulevard during a visit with my friend from high school, Rick Carr, a 4:03 miler for the University of Southern California. In Igloi's eyes, these were not extreme workouts but normal ones. Afterwards I experienced my worst-ever calf soreness, which convinced me not to return for a second day.

10 x 440 in 60-62 with 1 minute timed rest. This turned out to be a race disguised as a workout, because I ran it with an accomplished 22-year-old half-miler 10 years my junior, who wanted to demonstrate his superiority. I ran shoulder to shoulder with him, but it wore me out and trashed my next race. It was much too anaerobic.

40 x 220 in 31-33 with 220 jog after each. In the summer of 1968, I did severe damage to my Achilles tendons by running this workout 20 times over a two-month period. I ran them in spikes on a rock-hard cinder track and did not take easy days between these workouts. I also ignored the signals, extreme soreness in the tendons. The injury became chronic, lasting for years.

Up and Down Mount Scott. I ran up and down Mount Scott near Lawton in a burst of enthusiasm in my first summer of running. The road on which tourists drive to reach the top of the mountain rises 980 feet in a distance of 3 miles. I ran up and down it solo after running 12 miles at an easy pace from my home in Lawton. Fortunately, I somehow knew not to run hard going down the mountain, so I suffered no injury doing it. I recall that this workout was inspired by reading about the 200-mile-per-week training of Gerry Lindgren, the Washington State phenom who at age 19 ran 27:11.6 in the six mile, a world record.

Running fast over long downhill stretches can cause extreme muscle damage. In running, the leg muscles lengthen against their force (eccentric contractions) when the runner touches down on descent from each stride. Eccentric contractions are beneficial in strengthening a muscle, but only if the damage is slight and repairable before the next bout of exercise. Running downhill increases the time, terminal velocity, and impact force of the descent from each leap. This results in greater muscle damage than running on the flat. Ultra-marathoners, who typically compete on mountainous courses, can easily damage their fast-twitch muscle fibers with high mileage runs even though their pace is aerobic.

Bill Fornoff's Delayed Brush With Death

A few years ago, Bill Fornoff, a friend who was then 50 years old, ran the Western States 100 Mile Endurance Run, a race with 23,000 feet of descent. He finished it in just under 30 hours, overjoyed but fatigued.

"I felt so good about finishing I was crying," he recalled. But three days later after his flight home, he was in intensive care in a Baltimore hospital, battling the delayed effects of the muscle damage. His kidneys had shut down, clogged by the debris from his muscles in his bloodstream.

"I began to feel bad about eight hours after the race," he explained. "By Tuesday (two days later), I was one sick dog." A veteran of 10 ultramarathons and 45 marathons, he had gone through intensive preparation for the 100-miler and had run it properly, drinking frequently and maintaining his weight throughout the race. He spent 17 days in the hospital, seven of them in intensive care. He underwent five dialysis treatments and had a long recovery period afterwards. His experience illustrates the dangers of excessive downhill running.

Ryan Hall, America's best marathoner in 2011, had a similarly bad experience with an experimental workout of repeated down-the-mountain dashes, as reported by the *New York Times*.[27]

> *"Sprinting seven miles down a 9,000-foot mountain and then running back up to do it again may not appeal to even the most self-punishing of athletes, but Ryan Hall believes it is the kind of 'experimental workout' that transformed him into the fastest American distance runner in history. It is also the kind of extreme training that is now driving him to abruptly retire, two decades into an audacious career that produced national milestones—his time of 2 hours 4 minutes 58 seconds at the 2011 Boston Marathon is by far the fastest for an American runner....Hall, 33, who was one of the last remaining hopes for an American front-runner in this summer's Olympic marathon, is succumbing to chronically low testosterone levels and fatigue so extreme, he says, that he can barely log 12 easy miles a week."*

A year later, Hall was still unable to race: "I won't be trying to run fast anymore. I'll just enjoy myself and have fun."[28]

Each seven-mile downhill sprint was an imperfect workout because he repeated the downhill sprint when weakened from the previous downhill sprint.

It is easy to achieve an imperfect workout, but how difficult is it to achieve a perfect, or near-perfect workout? It is not easy for several reasons. First, the runner's pain feedback is not always delivered in real-time; muscle soreness is usually delayed 24 hours. Also, pain is not always proportional to damage, and damage potential varies with many factors. What may be the best way to achieve near-perfect workouts is to err on the easy side and finish feeling exhilarated, the approach the great Oregon coach Bill Bowerman employed.

Four-time Olympic champion Emil Zatopek routinely relied on what could be described as killer workouts. He improved with them between the 1948 and 1952 Olympic Games. But the wear and tear of the workouts eventually caught up with him as he trained for his third Olympic Games. He was running daily interval workouts of 100 x 400 meters, just as he had done in the previous year. But in 1956, at age 32, he sustained a groin injury, indicating that his work-rest balance point may have shifted over time. He was hospitalized for six weeks and resumed training the day after he left the hospital. He never regained his championship form and finished sixth in the 1956 Olympic marathon in 2:29:34–about 6 minutes slower than his winning time in 1952.

Sprinters' Approach for Near-Perfect Workouts

Examples of near-perfect workouts are those of the world's fastest sprinter, the cheetah. The cheetah is the world's fastest land animal because of its large quantity of fast-glycolytic muscle fibers, the most powerful but most easily damaged type of muscle fiber. These are the same fast-glycolytic muscles human runners possess in smaller proportions. The cheetah also has exceptional biological springs that enable it to accelerate from zero to 60 mph in 3 seconds and to hit top speeds of 60 to 70 mph. Its burst of speed may cover only 200 to 400 meters, but the damage potential in redirecting its kinetic energy in quick changes of direction during its pursuits is substantial. Fortunately, the cheetah is not pressed into racing for the entertainment and profit of human beings. In the wild, a lame cheetah is soon to die.

Cheetahs "train" instinctively (intuitively). After a successful dash to acquire a meal, the male cheetah is unlikely to sprint again for two to five days, resting until the feast is consumed and hunger returns. With too little rest, injuries would be more likely to occur, particularly to the cheetah's hamstring muscles, a common point of injury among human sprinters and greyhound racers. Females, who must feed their cubs, may sprint somewhat more frequently.

How has the cheetah managed to survive for 10,000 years since the last extinction event? By instinctively taking adequate recovery time following every top-speed sprint.

In college we distance runners used to joke about the sprinters' lower standards for workout density and intensity. I would sometimes see a sprinter run a complete workout of only 10 x 30-yard starts out of the blocks. If these speedsters had exposure to injury, it wasn't because of overtraining. It was in having to run three or four events—dashes and relay legs—per meet.

Adolph Plummer, a star sprinter at the University of New Mexico could have set the standard for success on light and infrequent workouts. At age 25, he broke the world record in the 440-yard dash on a cinder track at Arizona State University, running 44.9 and slicing 8 tenths off the world record. That's 44.6 for 400 meters. He later ran a 440-yard relay anchor in 44.4. He was truly a natural quarter miler. His teammate Pete Brown described one of the few workouts Plummer chose to attend in 1963, the year he broke the world record: "Workouts were, for the most part, a place where a captive audience was bombarded by an endless stream of (Adolph's) New York style quips and jokes."[29]

Like Cutting a Diamond

Training a sprinter is like cutting a diamond. Enhance its natural brilliance, improve its shape, but be careful not to break it.

Jesse Owens, arguably the greatest sprinter of all time, was discovered by Charles Riley, a physical education teacher, on a junior high school playground in Cleveland in 1928. Riley coached Owens until he enrolled in Ohio State five years later, focusing on efficient mechanics, perfect technique for sprint starts, and relaxed, precise running form. It is noteworthy that Riley's motto in training Owens was, "Train for four years from Friday," emphasizing patient long-term development rather than attempting to achieve quick results.

As such, his workouts could be described as near-perfect. They laid the foundation for two of the greatest achievements in track and field history. At the 1935 Big-10 Track and Field Championships he set world records in three events and tied the world record in a fourth in the span of 45 minutes. Fifteen months later, he won four gold medals in the Olympic Games in Berlin, setting world records in three events and tying the world record in the fourth.

A patient approach, avoiding imperfect workouts and the setbacks they cause, can lead to success for any runner. The potential point of injury is not just the hamstring, but all the muscles of the power train, particularly those below the knee when subjected to workouts or races so severe that recovery is outside the bounds of normal work-and-recovery cycles.

From the time I began to improve in my first year of running, when I perceived a path to perfection in running, I trained empirically. If the workout I decided to do was 40 times 220 yards in 33 seconds with a 220 walk-jog after each, I would do it to perfection. I wouldn't stop after 20 reps or slow down to 37 seconds. My psyche wouldn't permit such imperfections.

Subconsciously, I believed these workouts were perfect for me. Because the world-record-setters I chose as role models ran such workouts, I felt certain they were the best path to success. I couldn't run only 10 quarter-miles in a workout, I needed to run 14, 16, or 20. The problem, of course, is that I picked the wrong role models. Perfectionism in overly ambitious workouts and race frequency, as I now realize, was what prevented me from achieving my goal of sub-4.

In the second phase of my running life, road-racing with catch-as-catch-can training, perfectionism at times became hazardous.

Chapter Thirteen

Interval training and the heart

I take pride in having reached the threshold of the sub-4 mile with a progression similar to Roger Bannister's. In 1953, he ran 4:02.0 seven years after he first dipped under 5 minutes in the mile. In 1972, I ran 4:02.1, seven years after I first reached the novice milestone of a 5-minute mile. Here are our progressions:

Age	Bannister	Blewett
17	4:53.0	4:58.0
18	4:24.6	4:23.9
19	4:17.2	4:15.6
20	4:11.1	4:11.8
21	4:09.9	4:07.8
22	4:07.8	4:04.8
23	4:03.6	4:04.5
24	4:02.0	4:02.1
25	3:58.8	4:03.8

His goal of course was to be the first man to break 4:00. My goal of sub-4 evolved simply from an adolescent daydream. From my starting point in 1965, achieving sub-4 was as improbable as being the first man to walk on the moon. But the same thing can be said of countless young dreamers when they first go out for track in high school. I had no clue at the time whether I had the talent to do it, but over the next few years, I would learn about the science-based training method that would bring out this talent. The method was interval training.

Why did my performance diverge from Bannister's after the threshold year? I believe it was differences in racing and training in that pivotal year, which was my eighth year of training, 1973. Bannister always trained intuitively and honed his interval workouts in 1953 and '54 based on expert advice he received from Franz Stampfl, who helped him optimize his variables of interval training.

I, however, lost my focus on the mile, distracted by success in longer races that required more rest and recovery time than I allowed myself.

Simply running interval workouts was not a sure path to success. Kenny Moore reinforced this in my mind with what he wrote about interval training in his book, *Bowerman and the Men of Oregon*.

> *"Interval training takes such care that to this day few coaches can consistently produce milers. As he (Bowerman) timed them on interval days, he would scrutinize their form, grabbing a runner's throat and taking his pulse. He'd check the glint in their eye, sending the tight and dull to the showers and especially those whose pulses weren't quick to return to 120 beats per minute."*

He knew interval training to be a double-edged sword. It can bring rapid improvement, or it can produce injury or stagnation. The countless variables that affect how the human body responds to training make it difficult to achieve a perfect balance between stress and recovery, to find the optimal intensity between under-training and overtraining.

It was my good fortune to have been introduced to interval training in a beneficial form early in my running career, and it was my misfortune to have made frequent mistakes in my learn-by-doing period of self-coaching. In my eagerness to improve, I too often ran interval workouts that were imperfect or poorly sequenced in my cycles of training.

My first interval workouts

I ran my first interval workout on my first day of high school track practice in 1965. The workout—3 x 1320 yards in about 4 minutes with 15 to 20 minutes rest after each—was prescribed by my coaches, who did not explain why it was considered a good workout. The coaches were intent on getting us ready to race, not on teaching us the science of runner training. We did not begin with long slow distance running, building a base, as many coaches specify. We went straight to interval, and the reason—rapid improvement—soon became apparent, although I did not know much about improvement rate, rapid or otherwise, until months later.

My typical high school workouts were 8 x 440 in 70 seconds with a 440 walk in 5 minutes for rest after each; 30 x 110 yards with a 110 walk for rest; 9 x 220 in 29-32 seconds with a 220 walk for rest; 10 x 150 with a 150 walk (the workout we usually ran two days before a meet). The longer rest periods were neither typical nor optimal, but they were about right for me as a novice. About two-thirds of our workouts were interval and one-third slow distance on the grass.

Interval was also my first workout with the University of Oklahoma cross-country team on a 98-degree late-summer day in 1965. We ran six times a half-mile in 2:35 with a 3-minute rest after each, mostly under a row of shade trees in the park surrounding the campus duck pond. Over the next three days, the temperature peaked between 99 and 102 degrees when we ran our afternoon workouts—each involving repeat 440s or 880s. On the sixth day we ran a slow, steady 6-miler on the course, and on the seventh day, we rested. The pain or fatigue I feared might keep me from making the OU cross-country team never manifested.

In this freshman cross-country season, I was awed by the faster pace I could maintain almost effortlessly in workouts and time trials. Relative to my high school workouts, the repetitions were generally longer, larger in number, and shorter in rest interval—such as 16 x 440 in 72 to 75 with a 1-minute rest. In the second week of cross-country, I broke 5 minutes for the mile for the first time in a time trial. I was elated. By the end of my freshman year, eight months later, I had run 4:23.9 in a time trial on the track.

Interval, interval, interval. I ran hundreds of interval workouts in college. I did hundreds more after I left college because they worked so well when I ran them the way my coach, J.D. Martin, prescribed. I gained huge benefit in running intervals at threshold pace, at or near the anaerobic threshold, a pace at which lactate accumulates only to the point that it can be cleared during the rest period. I learned that the quantity we ran in college was about right, as was the pace, rest period, and frequency (three interval workouts per week on average). I did not know then why they worked so well, and I wasn't concerned about knowing why, as long as I was improving.

I was still running interval workouts two or three times a week as I approached age 75. That makes 57 years of interval training, probably some kind of record. Among the training methods I tried, interval done properly had the most positive effect on my development. Being self-coached after college, I did not always get it right, probably never got it perfect, but I was close to perfect in workouts once I learned the science of interval and how to manage its variables—exertion level, length of repetitions, number of repetitions, length of rest interval, frequency of interval workouts, progression in intensity, and the mode of active rest between interval days. There were times when I ran more than three interval workouts per week, but I found that for me, three was the practical limit.

When I read Fred Wilt's books, *Run, Run, Run,* and *How they Train,* and started reading research papers about the adaptations of exercise, I began to understand the scientific basis of interval training. It took many years, however, for me to fully understand the best practical application of interval training, its benefits and limitations.

Interval Training for Greater Heart Power

As a beginner in running, I did not know that it was important for a runner to have a powerful heart. Nor did I have reason to believe my heart was more powerful than normal. When I started running, it was surely not. But once I began interval workouts in high school, then in college, I learned the importance, and the power of my heart increased steadily as indicated by improved performance in races and workouts.

The main effect of interval training is to make the heart a more powerful pump capable of transporting oxygen-rich blood at high volume to the working muscles. Interval training does this by strengthening and stretching the heart, specifically the left ventricle of the heart, the chamber that pumps blood throughout the body. These are important adaptations not just for middle- and long-distance runners, but also for sprinters.

The human body runs on fuel and oxygen, as does the engine of an automobile. In your car's engine (the power-plant), the fuel and oxygen are brought together efficiently in each of the four, six, or eight cylinders for combustion. In the human body, fuel and oxygen are brought together efficiently in millions of microscopic power-plants called mitochondria within the muscle fibers. Mitochondria are about the size of bacteria.

In the automobile, fuel is stored as close to the engine as is safely possible, like the coal car of a steam locomotive, but oxygen must be drawn from the environment. In the human body, the main fuel for running (glycogen) is stored in the muscle fibers very close—within a micron or two of the mitochondria. Close storage of fuel makes the power plants very responsive for rapid start and acceleration.

For high levels of aerobic power, the runner must deliver oxygen to the muscle fibers at a rate much higher than normal through the lungs, heart, and blood vessels. This flow of oxygen is driven by two pumps —the lungs and the heart. When a trained athlete runs fast, the flow rate at which the heart pumps blood increases to as much as eight times the resting rate. The automotive analogy for delivering oxygen at very high flow rates for greater power is the turbocharger, which draws in great volumes of air and forces it into the cylinders. The heart is its own turbocharger and can adapt through training to achieve much higher flow rates of oxygen-rich blood. In startup, oxygen flow cannot be accelerated as rapidly as the fuel, so a limited amount of oxygen is stored temporarily inside each muscle fiber on transport molecules called myoglobin. Startup and acceleration occur with anaerobic power (oxygen not required) until the oxygen is fully available to the mitochondria.

The Most Powerful Heart in Racing

Perhaps the best example of a powerful heart in an athlete is that of a famous middle-distance runner whose image graced the covers of *Time, Sports Illustrated, and Newsweek* magazines in 1973. The secret of this runner's great success was revealed after his death 16 years later when his chest was opened for necropsy. He possessed the largest— and by inference the most powerful—heart ever seen in the world of racing. "We just stood there in stunned silence. We couldn't believe it. The heart was perfect. It was just this huge engine," said Dr. Thomas Swerczek, who performed the necropsy on this runner, the thoroughbred Secretariat.[30]

In the realm of horse racing, the revelation about Secretariat's heart was as stunning as his famous stretch run in winning the 1.5-mile Belmont Stakes, the third leg of the Triple Crown, by a record 31 lengths. The heart was estimated to weigh 22 pounds, making the ratio of his heart weight to his total weight (1,130 pounds racing weight) 1.8 percent. Across all animal species including horses and humans, the weight of the heart, which is mostly muscle, averages about 0.6 percent of body weight. Secretariat's heart was three times larger than that of a normal horse. His heart may have increased in size with training, but genetic research indicates that his large heart trait may have been a mutation that came down a genetic trail from a mare named Pocahontas.[31]

It is not known whether elite athletes of the human variety have ever developed hearts three times normal in size. Steve Prefontaine, who in 1972 set the American record in the 5,000 meters and placed fourth in the Olympics, was found to have a heart about 30 to 40 percent larger than that of an average man of equal age, height, and weight. His heart was about 1.2 liters in volume.[32]

By measuring heart dimensions with high-resolution echocardiography, a 1986 study of more than 1,000 competitive athletes found that their hearts were consistently larger than those of non-athletes—about 10 percent larger in dimensions of the left ventricle, 45 percent greater in mass of the left ventricle, and 15 to 20 percent greater in wall thickness.[33]

Changes to the mass and dimensions of the heart caused by repetitive exercise result in what's known as *athletic heart syndrome*. To achieve a powerful athletic heart requires increasing both the volume of the left ventricle and the thickness of the heart walls proportionally. For increased pumping power, there must be both.

There is scientific evidence that athletes in dynamic sports, such as running, are likely to develop increases in the maximum volume—the internal chamber diameter of the left ventricle—and that wall thickness will increase in proportion. In strength training, however, it is more likely that the wall thickness will increase without an increase in the diameter of the ventricle.[34]

Interval's First Success: 400- and 800-Meter World Records

The effects of interval training on the heart were first recognized in the 1930s by Dr. Woldemar Gerschler of Germany, who pioneered interval training and demonstrated its effectiveness in coaching Rudolph Harbig to world records in the 400 meters (46.0 seconds) and 800 meters (1:46.6) in 1939. Gerschler worked with a cardiologist named Herbert Reindel in many experiments on interval training and coached

Josy Barthel, the 1952 Olympic champion in the 1500 meters (3:44.1). Roger Bannister, who finished fourth, less than a second behind Barthel in the Olympics, began including intervals in his training after talking with Gerschler. In 1953, Bannister was introduced to Franz Stampfl, who had learned from Gerschler and had developed his own interval training system. Stampfl advised Bannister on interval training for several months before his 3:59.4 mile. It was apparently interval training that facilitated the 2.6-second improvement in Bannister's final year of running the mile.

Gerschler devised the following rule of thumb for the rest interval relative to the pace of the repetitions. The heart rate should drop from a range of 170-180 beats per minute to 120 beats per minute in the 1.5-minute rest period, and the interval training session should be terminated once the pulse recovery begins to take more than 1.5 minutes. These values were for repetitions of 200 to 400 meters, which Gerschler favored.

The 50-to-60 beat-per-minute drop in pulse rate is a good indicator that beneficial effects on the heart can be achieved without extreme intensity causing high lactate buildup or long duration workouts that increase the potential for leg injuries. It is thus an efficient way to improve the power of the heart and the VO2max. Stampfl knew this and asserted that *running faster than racing speed in workouts was not required*. When Bannister began running his 10 x 400-meter interval workouts in 66 seconds six months before breaking 4-minutes for the first time, it may have been due to Stampfl's influence, although Bannister was always intuitive in his training. By limiting the length of repetitions to the range of 200 to 400 meters, the runner can also develop the coordination for running at race pace without running highly anaerobic workouts and increasing the risk of injury.

The length of the rest period depends on pace and distance of the repetitions. My experience in running 10 x 400 at 60 to 62 seconds with 60 seconds rest proved to me the disadvantage of running repetitions at near race pace with too-short a rest interval. Even though I was in prime condition for racing when I ran this workout, my pulse dropped very little in just 60 seconds of rest at this pace. In contrast, in a workout of 10 x 400 in 70 seconds with 60 seconds rest, my pulse rate dropped nicely and there was no lactate accumulation for the duration of the workout. Running 20 x 200 in 30 seconds with a 90 second rest would have been at my mile race pace and at the appropriate workout intensity. Because the repetitions were just 200 meters in length, the workout was not highly anaerobic.

It is easy for an inexperienced runner to believe, falsely, that a painful, highly anaerobic interval workout will yield more rapid improvement. This is the harder-is-better perception, which can be very difficult to disprove and dislodge from the brain of runners who have experienced that approach. But as Gerschler, Stampfl, and Bannister found long ago, it is important that the variables of interval training be personally optimized for each runner using the simple rule of thumb on declining pulse rate.

How the Heart Stretches

Stroke volume is the quantity of blood ejected from the heart with each beat. Power is the stroke volume multiplied by the pulse rate. A heart with a high stroke volume beats more slowly than one of average stroke volume, because it requires fewer fillings of the ventricles to move the body's approximately 5 liters of blood through the system of blood vessels.

Per *The Textbook of Work Physiology*, "the individual with a high capacity for oxygen transport because of natural endowment and/or training is characterized by a large stroke volume and a slow heart rate.[35]" Taken upon awakening in the morning when resting, not immediately after an exertion or stress, the basal rate is a simple indication of a heart's stroke volume and pumping power. Ron Clarke, the Australian who set 17 world records in distance events, is said to have had a basal pulse rate of 28. My basal rate was 38 in my racing prime, and at age 75 it was still about 56. For an untrained person the basal heart rate can vary between 60 and 100 beats per minute.

The stimuli for stretching and strengthening the heart occur during and immediately after the rest interval. Stretching occurs in starting each repetition. Strengthening occurs in the stopping.

In beginning a race or repetition in a workout, the output of the heart increases as the working muscles' demand for oxygen increases with the runner's pace. In accelerating, the left ventricle stretches slightly more with each beat according to what's known as the Frank-Starling Law, which states that the stroke volume increases in response to an increase in the volume of blood in the ventricles. A larger volume of blood returns to the heart with increased velocity with each successive beat, filling the ventricle more quickly and stretching the muscle fibers further. The biological spring titin in the heart muscle stores and returns energy to amplify the power of its contraction. The pulse rate increases more quickly than the stroke volume.

In those not trained as runners, the stretching levels off at about half of VO2max; for trained runners it may increase to 100 percent of VO2max. This increases both the stroke volume and the force of contraction until they reach their maximums for a given blood volume and level of exertion. The arteries and veins, which are elastic, also stretch in diameter to accommodate the increasing flow rate.

Wearing a heart rate monitor while running intervals, a runner can see evidence of the stretching in the real-time heart rate; that is, in increasing the speed of the repetition, the pulse rate will increase then drop back even though the pace is faster than the previous repetition.

The stretching that occurs in the beginning of each run or repetition is temporary, but through a process called remodeling, which for the heart muscle involves adding muscle sarcomeres in series and myofibrils in parallel, it becomes semi-permanent. Like all other adaptations induced by training, they reverse when routine training ceases for a period of time, although significant enlargement of the heart has been found to persist in about 20 percent of retired and detrained elite athletes after more than five years.[36]

How the Heart Strengthens

Studying in my dorm room one evening in my sophomore year at OU, I noticed my heart was skipping beats at random times. I later noticed this skipping between repetitions of interval workouts. I made note of this in my running logbook and wondered if my heart was defective. I felt nothing unusual when these occurred, no light headedness or shortness of breath, and I had routinely submitted to physical exams, each of which showed my heart to be normal.

They continued for years, and I finally determined what caused them when I was in my 60s, still running two or three interval workouts per week, though much less intense ones, and still feeling the skipped beats. I searched the literature, finally determining that they were pressure-induced, occurring when the heart's brief isovolumic period—the interval that occurs briefly (normally 0.05 second) when pressure in the ventricle is increasing and all the valves are closed simultaneously.

The skipped beats are caused by an out-of-sync pressure pulse from the expansion and contraction of the aorta, the large, elastic artery, sometimes referred to as the fifth chamber of the heart, into which blood is ejected from the left ventricle. The aorta is the cushioning chamber of the heart, smoothing the pulsations of the heart beats. A normally elastic aorta stores about half the stroke volume during the heart's contraction (the systolic phase) then propels it through the body when the heart expands (the diastolic phase) ensuring a steady perfusion of all the organs.

Skipped beats begin during the rest period between repetitions when the stroke volume and heart rate are still higher than normal. With the pulse dropping rapidly and the aorta still expanding and contracting strongly, a mis-timed pressure pulse is sent toward and away from the heart, closing the aortic valve briefly before the left ventricle has fully completed its contraction. When this valve closes early, there is briefly no path for the blood to exit the left ventricle, and for an instant, it assumes a constant volume, like a water balloon being squeezed. This forces the heart muscle into an isometric contraction and for some of its muscle fibers, an eccentric contraction—lengthening against the muscle fibers' force. This amounts to an isometric resistance exercise for the cardiac muscle, strength-building with many brief repetitions.

These changes in heart rhythm do not show up on all pulse-rate monitors because they are pressure-induced, not electrically induced. Easily detectable by placing a finger on the pulse, the isovolumic beats are perceived as skipped beats or as more forceful beats, depending on where in the cycle of each beat the out-of-sync valve closing occurs.

How Rapidly is Greater Pumping Power Achieved?

Interval training can produce substantial improvements in aerobic power fairly rapidly. Experiments done in Germany in the late 1950s found that interval training increased the heart volume by more than 100 milliliters in about 3 to 8 weeks—for example, increasing a heart of 200-milliliter volume to 300 milliliters. Such an increase might take several months, even years with other approaches to training.[37]

World-record-setters Jim Ryun and Paula Radcliffe, whose VO2max test results are described in chapters 9 and 16, attained their highest level of VO2max very rapidly once they began serious training. Ryun reached his maximum in no more than three years. Marathon record holder Paula Radcliffe did so in her second year. For both of these high responders, their first-year performances indicate remarkably rapid improvement.

Interval is superior to long, slow distance running because of the two stimuli that occur during or immediately after the rest period. No matter what the distance, the steady-paced runs present the stimuli less frequently per workout, only at the beginning and end or upon ascending and descending hills. With steady, continuous runs, the pace is slower than that of interval repetitions, so the stroke volume and the stretching are likely to be less powerful.

In jogging between reps, it is similar to but more structured than fartlek, also known as speed play. The long runs that Peter Snell did on the hilly Waitara course were more effective in building heart power than were the steady runs on flat courses because of the change in pace—accelerating then decelerating.

Most runners have the ability to increase their maximum rate of blood flow, though the maximum varies with training and genetics. High level exertion by a non-athlete can raise the heart's stroke volume only to about four times the resting rate, i.e. an increase from 5 liters per minute at rest to about 20. An elite endurance athlete can achieve much larger stroke-volume increases—going to 30 or 40 liters per minute from a resting rate of 5.

Interval Training is Beneficial Even For the Elderly

Interval training is the most effective, and most efficient in that it takes less work—less wear and tear on the legs and feet to increase aerobic power. It is also beneficial to people of virtually any age.

As I learned from my treadmill workouts after turning 70, even slow fully aerobic interval workouts can increase the power of the heart. This is supported by studies such as one conducted in Norway involving 27 participants of average age 75.5, each of whom had suffered a heart attack at least a year earlier. The participants performed workouts three times per week for 12 weeks, but the exercise to elevate their heart rates was uphill walking rather than running. Nine performed aerobic interval training, and nine, moderate continuous training. The interval training involved walking four 4-minute repetitions at 90 to 95 percent of peak heart rate on an inclined treadmill with rest intervals of 3 minutes of slower walking after each repetition. Each session lasted 38 minutes, including warmup and cool-down.

Over the 12 weeks, the interval-training group was able to increase the treadmill incline to 12 percent, while the continuous training group, maintaining 70 to 75 percent of peak heart rate for 47 minutes, increased the incline to only 4.7 percent on average.

The interval-trained group averaged 46 percent improvement in peak oxygen uptake, a 15 percent improvement in work economy, and other improvements, including left-ventricle remodeling, endothelial function, and quality of life.[38] The nine in the continuous (steady-paced) training showed much less improvement.

A similar study conducted a decade later in the Netherlands found significant improvements in physical fitness but less favorable results overall. Two groups of 10 heart failure patients of average age 64 performed two sessions per week on cycle ergometers. For the interval training group, each session involved 10 repetitions of 1 minute each at 90 percent workload with 2.5 minutes of active rest after each. The continuous training group cycled for 30 minutes at 60 to 75 percent workload in each semiweekly session. In comparing the results to the Norwegian study, the authors noted that the training characteristics (frequency, intensity, and duration) are important factors determining training responses.[39]

Not all people have equal ability to strengthen and stretch their hearts with interval training, however. Certain structural characteristics, not easily measurable, can limit the improvement. Some improve quickly; others slowly. A small or inelastic aortic arch probably does not provide the valve-closing counter-impulse a larger, more elastic aorta does.

One seemingly minor adaption that helps a runner attain maximum benefit from interval training is the increase in blood volume. Executed by the pituitary gland and kidneys, this adaptation facilitates an increased stroke volume and with it, increased stretching of the left ventricle. This is typically the first adaptation to occur, and it is brought on by training consistently. In untrained people, blood volume can increase by around 10 percent within the first day of training,[40] but the runner has to be properly hydrated to make it happen. With a smaller blood volume due to dehydration, there is less of a stimulus for stretching.

Interval training, done properly, is a key to success in racing and to better cardiovascular health. It requires intelligent experimentation to learn one's own optimal combination of variables at any given time relative to the sequence of workouts and races. It may not be easy to determine. It may take months or years to learn how to run interval workouts for best results. But it is worth the time and effort.

Chapter Fourteen
The trouble with doubles

The Drake Relays, held in Des Moines, Iowa, each spring, has long been a grand stage for competition among elite athletes and teams. Like other relay meets, it often requires collegiate runners to compete in two or more races in the meet. I competed in the Drake Relays in April 1969 and doubled in the distance medley relay and steeplechase with only one hour between them.

Jim Ryun also doubled at Drake that year, running the anchor leg for Kansas in the 4x1-mile relay on Friday and the sprint relay (440, 220, 220, and 880 yards) on Saturday. His was a fairly easy double, given the day of rest between his two races.

He had doubled in the Kansas Relays one week earlier, anchoring the 4x1-mile relay to victory and distance medley relay (880, 440, 1320, and mile) to a world record. He had given an all-out effort in front of his home crowd, then worked hard in practice the next few days. Consequently, he arrived at Drake tired, feeling he would be unable to run well. His condition became apparent in his first race when he ran a 4:11.6 on the anchor of the 4x1-mile. Then in the rain on Saturday in the sprint medley, a race with world-record possibilities, he slowed to a jog on the last lap and walked off the track.

He drew harsh reactions for quitting the race, as documented in an article in the *Des Moines Register* newspaper the following day. It illustrated the intense pressures Ryun faced in every race:

> "Jim Ryun shocked a rain-drenched throng at the Drake Relays Saturday by quitting halfway through the only race in which he was entered (in the Saturday session), saying

he was too tired to run. ... Reminded that he owed some explanation to the fans, many of whom sat through a steady downpour mainly to see him compete in the featured sprint medley, Ryun added: "Basically I was tired. Anything else will have to come from the coach. Let him tell you about it."...."Ryun owed these fans more than he gave them," said one disappointed official on the infield. "I hope he keeps running another year and comes back to run an open mile at Drake or he'll never have the fans here on his side again."[41]

He did not return to Drake. In better times, Ryun anchored the University of Kansas distance medley to a world record of 9:33.8 in the 1967 Drake Relays. Thirteen years earlier, Wes Santee ran a 4:07.4 anchor leg to propel Kansas to a world record of 9:50.4. He then ran a 1:51.6 anchor an hour later to secure a win in the 4x880. He also anchored wins in the sprint medley and the 4x1-mile in the two days of the meet. Three or four races per meet were the norm for Santee in the big relay meets. He was named the outstanding performer in the 1953 and 1954 Texas Relays for his multiple relay wins.

At Drake in 1954, Santee clashed with his coach Bill Easton about the heavy racing load, hoping instead to focus on running the mile fresh. His goal was to become the first runner to break 4 minutes in the mile—to beat Bannister and Landy to that historic achievement.[42] Sportswriters who saw his outstanding performances on the relay circuit opined that he had the ability to do it. Easton, a very knowledgeable and analytical coach, assured Santee there would be time later in the year for the assault on the 4-minute barrier. But first, he had to dominate the midwest relay circuit—the Kansas, Drake, and Texas Relays.

In 1969, my assignment at Drake was less demanding, and expectations were much lower when I ran a double—first, the mile leg on OU's distance medley relay then the 3,000-meter steeplechase. I was optimistic going into this prestigious meet. I had three recent run-like-a-deer races, all resulting in school records—a third-place finish in the 2-mile in 9:04.8 in the Big-8 Indoor Championships on the Kansas City track; a 14:13.5 three-mile in Dallas; and in the Texas Relays, a 4:07.8 mile leg on the distance medley, placing fifth with teammates Cline Johnson, Craig Wise and Marty McGeehee in 9:46.8, a school record.

* * *

A Most Memorable Double

Running on Drake's new all-weather urethane track in a light rain before a crowd of 18,000, our relay team finished sixth in the medley in 9:47.2, one place ahead of Kansas (without Ryun). My anchor-leg mile in the relay was ordinary, a 4:09.5, but my steeplechase performance one hour later was extraordinary in an unusual way.

The spectators were quiet in response to the second race of Ryun's double on that rainy day, but they were not silent in response to my second event, the steeplechase, a seven-and-a-half lap race that beats the life out of the legs with 28 three-foot-high rigid barriers and seven water jumps. The water jumps make the race popular with photographers, not so popular with the runners. It is a tough race to run fresh and a very tough race to run on a double with barely 60 minutes rest.

Feeling a bit heavy after my relay mile, I started the steeplechase at the rear of the pack, in nineteenth place among 19 runners. I was not paying close attention as we reached the first barrier. With 18 bodies obstructing my forward view, I didn't notice how rapidly I was approaching the barrier. Before I knew it, I had violated one of the rules of good hurdling: Never try to hurdle a barrier once your stomach is in contact with said barrier. With zero forward space in which to lift the lead leg and zero momentum, I had but two options, both clearly undesirable—crawl over or crawl under. The latter was contrary to the letter and spirit of the rules, so I chose the former. I placed both hands on the barrier and straddled it as if I were mounting a carnival pony bareback. Perhaps I thought no one would notice my doing this, but as the last runner in the pack, I was wrong, quite wrong.

Humor is said to be the juxtaposition of two incongruous thoughts. What my freestyle hurdling technique produced was the juxtaposition of two incongruous sights: a pack of 18 runners flowing smoothly over the barrier like a slinky on a staircase followed by a lone runner, me, cautiously mounting and dismounting with full crotch contact. Based on the full-throated roar that resulted, I believe all 18,000 spectators found it amusing. It was a roar like none I had ever heard before, or since.

I had no time to ponder whether the roar was actually for me or for some remarkable long-jump performance on the infield. I had six and three-quarters laps to go and was dropping five meters further behind the pack with each passing second.

My unintentional comedy was not yet complete. Each time I cleared another barrier, there was hearty applause, and when I finally passed the next-to-last runner, more applause. I felt it best not to acknowledge any of this applause with gestures that might imply a lack of serious intent (in violation of the Runner's Creed). I finished eighteenth among 19 in 9:58.7, one minute and two seconds behind the winner. Not quite lapped, I received a sitting ovation. Those Iowans showed a good sense of humor, and the announcer, a good sense of empathy and restraint. He avoided more laughter by not saying, "now finishing next to last, Bill Blewett." None of the officials spoke to me afterwards to say I owed the fans more than I gave them. Nor was I invited not to return the following year. Like Ryun, I did not return. I never ran another steeplechase.

Lost in all of this was a lesson about The Bear, the effect of lactate on running performance. The lesson was similar to Arthur Lydiard's admonition about excessive anaerobic running when we would meet a year later at the Astrodome. Neither lesson sank in until many years had passed.

Lactate Controls the Pace and the Recovery

Running more than one race per meet has long been the norm, particularly when team scores are kept in track meets, officially or informally. I often ran two races per meet throughout my track career, starting with the 880-yard run and a 440 leg on the mile relay in high school. In college my double was the mile and three-mile, and after college I doubled out of habit, not knowing that each double was a potential setback in my quest for sub-4. NCAA track teams no longer run dual and triangular meets as they did throughout much of the twentieth century, but running multiple races in a meet remains common in high school meets among two, three or four teams.

In high school, some coaches believe running multiple races per meet is beneficial for developing runners; it provides a workout more challenging than normal or one that allows one to turn four mediocre performances into a meet-winning ironman-like performance. For a runner with performance goals, however, a good thing it is not. It results in excessive anaerobic running, more encounters with The Bear, and lost opportunities for improvement in performance.

Thousands of scientific studies on lactate have been published since the year I ran my unforgettable steeplechase. Many of the studies have focused on the lactate threshold—also known as the point of maximal lactate steady state, the anaerobic threshold, and the onset of blood lactate accumulation. An excellent source of this information is the *Textbook of Work Physiology* fourth edition.[43] Its information on lactate would be very helpful to runners and coaches except that the audience for which the book is written consists of physiologists, clinicians, advanced students, and physical educators. It is not an easy read.

Lactate was once believed to be simply a waste product of the anaerobic metabolism. It is now understood to be an intermediate of the aerobic process, a partially spent fuel that can be transported from the muscle fiber in which it is produced to another muscle fiber to be used as a fuel, releasing what remains (about 92 percent) of its original energy.[44]

At high exertion levels, lactate accumulates very rapidly in the working muscles and, with a brief lag, it accumulates rapidly in the bloodstream. Data of a laboratory experiment graphed in the *Textbook of Work Physiology*, explains that the blood lactate concentration of an athlete running at 11.2 mph increased sixteen-fold in just 2 minutes of running and kept rising for 4 minutes after the running ceased, peaking at 25 times the initial concentration. The 4-minute rise afterwards occurs because of the time delay of passing out of the muscle fibers into the bloodstream. One hour later the concentration was still about three times higher than it was at rest.

In view of this data, it is likely that in my mile anchor leg at Drake, my lactate concentration rose to an even higher level than that measured in the lab experiment, and it took longer to return to the resting level. After an hour of recovery, my blood lactate was probably still above the resting value. If so, it was raising my concentrations above the lactate steady state level for which I was conditioned. This meant that in the steeplechase, The Bear would have climbed aboard much sooner if I tried to run the pace I was normally capable of. The race was thus destined to be a poor one, whether I bungled my first barrier crossing or not.

This data also implies that increasing lactate concentrations too much with anaerobic running in the warm-up before a race, for example running 200 meters well above race pace, can have a negative effect on race performance.

Had I known this outcome was likely, I would have tried to scratch from steeplechase. Looking back, I can recall only two instances in which I ran a personal best in the second race of a double. In both, I had at least 3 hours between the races, plenty of time for lactate to clear. My philosophy on racing was never to race unless I was 100 percent ready to race and that I should always *expect* to run like a deer. Doubling on short rest is clearly ill-advised.

Recovering More Quickly Between Races

Had I known about the existence and benefits of muscle pumps in my legs (explained further in Chapter 20), I could have achieved a more rapid recovery between races by walking or jogging slowly. Walking and jogging maintain a higher level of blood circulation to the legs and feet than does sitting or standing still. Walking, even at a slow pace, keeps the muscle pumps working. The one-way valves in veins of the legs pump blood by the squeezing action of the contracting muscles surrounding the veins, returning it from the feet to the heart. This hastens the clearing of the lactate by increasing the blood flow to and from the legs by about six fold, at a pace too slow to produce significant lactate.[45]

More rapid clearing of lactate can also be achieved with good conditioning. Interval training at the anaerobic threshold can increase the quantity of mitochondria and lactate transport molecules within the muscle fibers and increase the density of capillaries supporting the muscle fibers. The transport molecules enhance the ability to move lactate out of and into muscle fibers to improve the ability to sustain a higher level of power. The lactate can be used as fuel within the muscle fibers in which it is generated or be transported rapidly to enter another muscle fiber to be used as fuel. This improves the ability to clear lactate from the muscles and to make immediate, beneficial use of lactate.

The slow clearing of lactate is not the only adverse effect the first race has on the second. My first race at Drake surely consumed much of the glycogen in the leg muscles, leaving me more likely to fatigue earlier in the second race. When marathoners deplete their glycogen after running about 20 miles, their bodies switch to fats for fuel, which results in a reduced power output because of the increased oxygen requirement for oxidizing fat.

Drinking between races is also important, particularly in warm weather, to maintain blood volume to ensure aerobic power is not diminished in the second race. In middle-distance races, such a power loss can throw a runner out of contention; tactics for these races require maintaining contact. A runner cannot allow a large gap to open then expect to reel in the pack with a long kick as Dave Wottle did in winning the 800 meters in the 1972 Olympics. Normally a miler, Wottle felt that the first 200 meters in 24.9 seconds was much too fast so he held back, 10 meters behind the pack. By running a conservative pace, he avoided an early lactate build-up. Consequently, he did not allow The Bear aboard in the final lap, and he had ample power to come from behind. After his first lap in 52.9 seconds, he ran his second lap in 53.0 seconds and won by 3 hundredths in 1:45.9.

Another adverse effect of doubling is not being fully recovered for the next race on the calendar. After a double, there is unlikely to be a full restoration of glycogen to the leg muscles for the next race if it is just a week or less away, as is often the case during track season. This is due to the effect of muscle damage on glycogen restoration, as noted in chapter 4. Total glycogen depletion from the races of a double or just from the severe exertion of a single race and workouts that follow can affect the next race a week or more later.

When a race involves extensive muscle damage, as occurs in a marathon, running during the recovery period is of questionable benefit. A study published in 1984 compared the recovery of two groups of five runners after each ran a personal-best marathon. In the seven days after the marathon, one group did no training, just walking, while the other group ran 20 to 25 minutes per day at 50 to 60 percent of VO2max. The group that did no post-marathon training regained work capacity and muscle strength more quickly.[46]

High lactate concentrations in exercise are associated with greater muscle damage, though it is uncertain whether lactate *worsens* the muscle damage. In temporarily reducing the power of the muscles, high lactate levels can lead to injury through differential fatigue; that is, the fast-twitch muscles fatigue more rapidly than the slow-twitch causing a power imbalance in the propulsive chain of running.

Six days after Drake, I ran another double, a mile and 3-mile, in a dual meet against Oklahoma State. I ran poorly in the mile, finishing third with a deficient kick in 4:12.8. Afterwards, I won the 3-mile, but with a time of only 14:39.7. I next had disappointing performances in two 3-

mile races on the following two weekends to conclude my final collegiate season.

Doubling May Have Cost Santee a Historic First

Inconsistency in performance is known to be an indicator of overtraining or over-racing. The doubling-induced fatigue and inconsistency I was experiencing at Drake were probably similar to but less than Santee experienced in 1953 and 1954, when he was hoping to be the first man to break 4:00 in the mile.

In a meet in Compton, Calif. in June 1953, he broke the American record in the mile. After dawdling through a 2:05.2 first 880, he took the lead and finished with a 1:57.1 last 880 but struggled under the weight of The Bear the last 110 yards to finish in 4:02.4. Two weeks later he ran 4:03.7 and 1:50.8 for a double win in the NCAA Championships in Nebraska, and 10 days later, he won the National AAU mile in 4:07.6.

In the 1954 season, as his coach had assured him, he was given the opportunity to run an almost-fresh mile in the 1954 Kansas Relays. There, he set the Glenn Cunningham Mile record of 4:03.1. It surely would have been faster had a sudden thunderstorm not softened the cinder track. To make emergency repairs to improve the footing, there were only shovels and a small power roller—no steamroller.

Five weeks after Bannister ran his 3:59.4 in May 1954, Santee lowered his American record in the Missouri Valley AAU meet in Kansas City. Running fresh, he clocked 4:01.3, lowering by 1.1 seconds the record he had set a year earlier.

He had only two more chances to break 4:00 before he was to begin his military service with the Marine Corps. In a mile race in Compton, Calif., he passed the three-quarter-mile mark in 2:59.0 and reached the 1,500-meter mark in world record time, but he felt the weight of The Bear in the final straightway, slowing to a 4:21-mile pace over the last 120 yards to finish in 4:00.6. The following night in Stockton, Calif., he beat Olympic champion Josy Barthel with near-perfect pacing. He passed the three-quarter-mile mark in 3:00, but again lactate reduced his power as he exited the final turn. He finished in 4:00.7.

He had been competing at a high level for almost five months and was reported to be "plain tired out" and five pounds underweight. He was certainly in good enough form to break 4:00, but the busy collegiate season took precedence and never let him taper for a serious four-minute mile attempt." As he told the *University Daily Kansan*: "Having to compete for the university, I've run everything from soup to nuts. I haven't been permitted to concentrate."[47]

He would later run 4:00.5 in his last season, 1955, but the sub-4 mile he seemed certain to achieve ultimately eluded him. He missed sub-4 because of the heavy racing schedule and its effects that slowed his pace on the last lap or final straightaway. His racing schedule also had the subtle effect of crowding out potential opportunities to run a perfect race on a perfect track, in perfect weather, perfectly recovered from previous races—perfectly prepared for success.

Santee's was a cautionary tale that I did not understand until many years later—what Arthur Lydiard described as too much anaerobic running. Had his racing schedule been like Bannister's, two races a month with no doubling, he might have been the first to run sub-4.

As my final year of NCAA eligibility drew to a close, my future in racing was uncertain. But in looking back through the first four years of races and the workouts I had logged, I saw that despite inconsistency in the short cycles of my training, I had been consistently improving at a good rate, running personal bests every year.

Having studied the progression of outstanding runners whose training and racing I had tabulated for Fred Wilt, I felt confident that *if* I could find and sustain the right balance among workouts, races, and resting, I would continue to improve every year. It would be a challenge. I did not, however, find this balance in the next two years as I had hoped.

Chapter Fifteen
The phenomenon of running like a deer

The image of my left foot, barely noticeable in the corner of a framed black-and-white photograph, caught my attention as I walked past my bookcase one day. This 8x10 photo was my keepsake of ambivalence—a most-favorite photo taken during a least-favorite performance. It was taken in the mile race of the 1967 Big 8 Conference Track and Field Championships at OU, a very disappointing race. The photo, which depicted me running beside Jim Ryun, was a keeper, one to show the grandkids in remembrance of my running career, not specifically of the race it depicted.

I had expected to run like a deer that spring day in 1967, just as I had eight days earlier in the dual meet against Kansas. Why didn't I? Why were those painless, effortless, personal-best races so seldom repeated? Why weren't they available on demand? It was a mystery that I believe held the key to my breaking 4 minutes in the mile.

The 8x10 offered me a clue, though it came many years after I needed it. I had walked past it every day for at least 25 years before noticing that my left heel was on the ground just a quarter mile into the race. It was a bad sign. Neither I nor the world-record holder running beside me, nor any of the other runners in the meet were heel strikers.

What this image implied was that my calf muscles had become fatigued, making it impossible to maintain good, natural foot mechanics with which to recycle energy and amplify power via my Achilles tendons. For most of the race, I was temporarily a heel-striker. Was *this* the reason I ran so poorly that day?

After this chance observation, I began to search the literature for studies to quantify the effects of foot mechanics, specifically on mechanical efficiency—how biological springs store and return energy to make running more economical. I sought not only the science of the biological springs but also measures to ensure the springs always provided maximum benefit in races.

Like a Pogo Stick

Energy is the capacity to do work, and power is the rate of doing work. The biological springs in tendons, ligaments, and muscle fibers enable a runner to recycle the kinetic energy of each leap—running is a series of leaps—and to amplify the power applied to each leap. The springs make the runner faster and more efficient by briefly storing energy then releasing it more rapidly than the muscles have supplied it. It is the same principle applied for propulsion with the bow and arrow, sling shot, medieval catapult, trampoline, and pogo stick. As a fourth-grader I was an enthusiastic owner and operator of a pogo stick. I hopped with great joy, counting the number of hops by the thousands. I was indefatigable in my hopping because the heavy-duty steel spring returned almost all of the energy of each hop.

The runner's leg operates much like a pogo stick. Runners propel themselves forward and upward in a series of leaps, briefly storing energy in the biological springs when the leg is ahead of the body's center of gravity then returning that energy once the body's center of gravity has moved ahead of the leg. While working against gravity with each leap, the pogo stick can move in any direction by changing the angle in a similar way.

The Achilles tendon is the runner's heavy-duty spring. It amplifies power and lengthens the stride without requiring additional metabolic energy from the muscles. With natural foot mechanics, it increases efficiency by recycling about half of the energy invested in the upward phase of each leap. This is energy that would be lost in the descent from each leap if there were no biological springs to store and return the energy.

The springs provide a decisive advantage for athletes in many sports. Tendons connect muscle to bone. Ligaments connect bone to bone and have less importance than tendons in running. Collagen fibrils are in both tendons and ligaments. There are also millions of smaller springs, elastic molecules called titin, the longest protein chain in the body, within all the skeletal muscles. Titin fortifies muscle fibers, preventing each myofibril from being torn apart when the muscle fibers are stretched too far. All these springs in the legs collectively act to store and return energy.

Springs of elastic stiffness matched near-perfectly to one's body weight (i.e. tuned springs) enabled Spud Webb, a former professional basketball player, to slam dunk through a standard goal as a 5-foot-3-inch junior-high-school student. Superior tuned springs, along with excellent body control, enabled Javier Sotomayor of Cuba to set the world record of 8 feet in the high jump, 20 inches above his head. Well-tuned springs helped Jesse Owens set or tie world records in two dashes, a hurdle race, and the long jump in just a 45-minute span in the 1935 Big-10 Conference Track and Field Championships.

The Fastest Runner on Two (Skinny) Legs

The reigning king of spring among two-legged runners is the ostrich. We human runners are slow-movers compared to this big, flightless bird, whose long, elastic leg tendons provide a huge advantage in speed and endurance. The adult male of the species, which has NFL-lineman-like numbers for size—about 6 feet 10 inches tall and 300 pounds—but not for weight distribution, could run a mile in about 2 minutes and a half-marathon in about a half hour, if somehow incentivized to keep the pace up for 13 miles. It has a top speed of about 44 mph.

So what is the relevance of the ostrich to my phenomenon of running like a deer? I could have called it running like an ostrich, but neither the ostrich nor its running mechanics have the same beauty of motion as a deer. Both are very fast, and both have excellent springs. The springs of the ostrich enable it to cover up to 16 feet in a single stride. The deer runs with more air time, bouncing along at 30 to 35 mph and covering as much as 25 feet in a single leap from the hind legs to the forelegs. Running economy and power amplification are the obvious characteristics of running like either one.

The ostrich is superior to the best human runners in at least four attributes—the power of the upper leg muscles relative to body weight, the tidal volume of the lungs, which is about four to five times that of humans;[48] the pumping power of the heart, and the biological springs of its legs. It is a exceptional runner of great versatility.

The tendons of its legs and feet make it the fastest, most economical runner on two legs. Three tendons in each of its lower legs are almost three feet long, much longer than the human Achilles tendon, which is about 9 inches long. For a given thickness, the longer the tendon, the greater is the amount of energy it can store and return. One estimate is that ostriches store and return 83 percent more energy with their leg tendons than do humans; consequently, in running, the energy cost per kilogram of body mass for ostriches is estimated to be half that of humans.[49] Pound for pound, the ostrich uses less metabolic energy from the muscles; so, it fatigues less rapidly than it would without any springs.

Just as there is a huge difference between ostriches and people in the benefits of the biological springs, there are large differences among people. This difference occurs is in the elastic stiffness of the springs relative to the runner's weight, and the quality of the foot mechanics.

In foot mechanics there are three important avoidances that apply to runners—to avoid heel-striking, heel-dipping, and high foot-strike angles. These do not apply to the ostrich, which has digitigrade stance, standing on spring-loaded digits with raised metatarsal bones, somewhat like the human hand in fingertip pushups. The tendons of these digits contribute to its energy efficiency and power.

For human runners to gain the most benefit from the Achilles tendons, they must lock the muscles of the lower leg into isometric contractions just before landing from each leap. This is to cause all the stretching and energy storage *to occur in the Achilles tendon, not in the calf muscles*. The calf muscles must become unyielding, like a strut, until that foot leaves the ground.

The runner's foot should strike the ground at a low angle of about 15 degrees, and the heel should drop only about a centimeter—the amount the Achilles should stretch—once the forefoot is planted. It is best that the heel not touch the ground. Other plantigrade animals—those that walk on the soles of their feet, including Mallard ducks, run with the same ideal foot mechanics.

Neither ostriches nor ducks nor deer have to be taught good mechanics. They come naturally, of course, to these wild animals. They also come naturally to young children. Forefoot strike, foot angle, and heel stability are all natural when a child begins to run. "Young children usually possess wonderful running action. They have never been taught to run; they know nothing about style, yet they are often perfect stylists," wrote Franz Stampfl, one of the pioneers of interval training.[50] It is my observation that foot mechanics often change in adolescence with increased body mass without an attendant increase in strength and endurance of the calf muscles.

These natural mechanics are key to amplifying and transmitting the power to the ground for propulsion. Such are the foot mechanics of champion runners, from sprinters to marathoners. Most runners in collegiate competition and above, never have to be coached in foot mechanics because to reach that level of competition, they must have near-perfect foot mechanics. So what can go wrong?

Heel Dipping Wastes Energy and Power

Fatigue can cause even the best of runners, despite proper foot-strike angle, to succumb to heel dipping, with the heel dropping almost imperceptibly, or hitting the ground lightly, or hitting with full impact. This can occur near the end of a 100-meter dash, or near the end of a marathon once depletion of glycogen stores has reduced the power of the calf muscles, where the load on the muscles is the greatest. A gradual shift to heel dipping apparently caused by fatigue can be seen in a YouTube slow-motion video in which Usain Bolt wins a 100-meter dash. Bolt's heels never touch the ground over the 100 meters; he maintains perfect foot mechanics throughout the race. But the runners on either side, who are also very good sprinters, begin to drop the heels to the track in approaching the finish.

Not only can fatigue cause heel-dipping, but heel-dipping can cause fatigue. Another chance observation helped me understand the consequences of heel dipping. A few years ago, I coached a runner in his early 20s, who was fairly successful in road races from 5K to 10 miles. In one year, he won the Maryland-DC RRCA roadracing series. He had somehow learned at a younger age to run with a high foot angle, about 30 degrees, allowing a large heel dip controlled by the eccentric contraction of his calf muscles. I found that he was unable to maintain a constant pace or cadence for more than a quarter mile when running near his anaerobic threshold.

It was several months of observing his mechanics before I understood the reason for his inability to hold a steady cadence and pace. With the help of slow motion video, I saw that even at a jogging pace, his heels dipped more than an inch but never touched the ground. He had strong, rather large calf muscles, but the high foot angle and large heel drop caused his calf muscles to fatigue rapidly.

Consequently, it was almost impossible for him to run an even pace at speeds faster than a jog. In running half-mile repetitions at a moderate pace in a workout, for example, his cadence would drop from 185 strides per minute at the start to 165 at the finish. The heel dipping reduced the elastic stiffness of his legs, slowing his cadence, hastening fatigue, and minimizing his ability to recycle energy and maintain an even pace.

His foot mechanics, which were automatic and comfortable to him, provided better shock absorption than normal mechanics. This was a problem, however, because his calf muscles, not his Achilles tendons, were absorbing the kinetic energy of descent from each stride. The calf muscles thus acted as the main springs of his lower legs. As a biological spring, muscle is inferior to tendon. Muscle is a weaker spring. When a strong spring (the Achilles) is placed in series with a weak spring (the calf muscles), the weak spring is dominant in determining the elastic stiffness of the two. A runner's cadence is determined largely by the elastic stiffness of the legs, so as the calf muscles fatigue, the stiffness diminishes and cadence becomes steadily slower.

Seeing my protege's steady decline in cadence and pace confirmed what I was learning about my being able to run like a deer. Though my heel dipping was unintentional and often imperceptible, I was absorbing kinetic energy of the leaps in my calf muscles. This resulted in compounding of fatigue, slower cadence, slower pace, less energy efficiency, less power amplification, and next day soreness in the calf muscles that would delay the restoration of glycogen. My calf muscles became sore after every mile race.

In heel-dipping, I was wasting the available energy that could have been recycled, and in the latter part of the race, I was a very uneconomical runner.

Bill Rodgers' Excellent Economy

In the summer of 1974, I raced a mile in a track meet in Boston. As I waited to warm up for my race, I watched a runner finish the 10,000 meters. He was lapping the field, but what struck me and stuck in my memory was not his huge lead but rather the ease, the economy with which he was speeding around the track. This was, for me, a striking you-know-it-when-you-see-it revelation about the benefits of the biological springs. He was gliding, his lead implying the huge advantage he gained from his springs. The runner's name, previously unknown to me, was Bill Rodgers. This race occurred a year before he emerged as America's best marathoner. In 1975, He won the Boston Marathon in 2:09:55, a new American record. He went on to win the New York City Marathon and the Boston Marathon four times each. I later read that his VO2max was lower than most other world-class marathon runners, confirming in my mind that he was exceptionally economical, getting more power for less metabolic energy than other elite runners.

Four years later, I ran against him in the Cherry Blossom 10-mile in Washington, D.C., on a very windy day. The first 5 miles were downwind, and the last 5, upwind. When we made the turn into the wind at the five-mile point in 24:30, there were four of us in the lead pack. I looked to my right, and there was Bill Rodgers. He then appeared to gradually accelerate, but in reality, I was decelerating against the resistance of the wind. He very smoothly held his pace, however, leaving behind me and the others, who were less economical. I ran my last five miles in 25:50, and he, in 24:25 . He won in 48:55. I finished eighth in 50:20.

There's more to this story about economy. In the 10,000-meter final of the 1976 Olympic trials, Rogers aggravated an injury to the ball of his right foot. It did not heal completely before the Olympic Marathon in Montreal, in which he was clearly one of the favorites. He took the lead and pushed the early pace but finished fortieth in 2:25:14 behind the winning time of 2:09:55 by the East German runner Waldemar Cierpinski. The pain in the foot apparently affected his mechanics, upsetting the fine tuning of his springs. He explained how his race went badly in his book, *Marathon Man*.[51]

"After six miles into the race I felt ...none of the fluidity of each stride....my body was working harder than it should have been. My muscle energy wasn't being distributed in a normal way....My right leg was doing much more work than it was used to."

Heat and dehydration—it was 77 degrees and humid—were also factors in the race, but such conditions would have given the most economical runner an advantage. It seemed obvious to me that the foot injury reduced his mechanical efficiency, keeping him from running like a deer, as he normally did.

The ability to sustain ideal foot mechanics is of great importance in races of any distance. In my races, long or short, it became apparent that recovery from muscle damage and depletion from the previous race was key to restoring full mechanical efficiency for a race. If I cut short my recovery period, resumed intense training too quickly, my heels would dip at some point in the next race, imperceptibly at first and more as calf-muscle fatigue worsened. As Dr. David Costill wrote: "the rate of recovery from an exhaustive competition depends to a large degree on the amount of muscle trauma and glycogen depletion experienced during the race."[52]

I believe I ran like a deer only when the following were true on race day:

- Muscle damage was fully repaired.
- Glycogen was fully restored to all the muscles that power the run, particularly the muscles most abused in races, those of the lower leg.
- Achilles tendons were free of inflammation and soreness.
- Blood volume was fully restored with proper hydration.

Deer are blessed with lots of spring, which bestows great speed and endurance, reliably not randomly, because deer run on hooves. They don't have to lock-in proper foot angles and keep heels, which they don't have, vertically stable with muscle contractions. If their biological springs were optimal in their service only occasionally, as mine were, deer would have long ago perished from the earth. The same is true for ostriches, cheetahs, and other animals that survive on speed.

I felt I had finally learned the secret of running like a deer and how to ensure that I could experience this phenomenon in every race, not just randomly and infrequently. Though the power boost of my springs was much less than that of a deer, it was surely worth at least the 2 1/2 seconds I needed to better 4:00 in the mile. This realization, however, came too late. My racing days had long since ended.

Chapter Sixteen

What I didn't know: how to rise from a plateau

Leonard Hilton was the first native Texan to run a sub-4 mile. I competed against him several times in college, outran him once or twice, and got to know him. His success gave me encouragement in my goal of sub-4. In 1972 he made the U.S. Olympic team in the 5,000 meters, having finished third in the trials behind Steve Prefontaine. In 1973, he ran a personal best mile of 3:55.9. Three years earlier, he anchored his University of Houston distance medley team to an indoor world record.

In May of 1973, when I was living in the Northeast Texas town of New Boston, Leonard invited me to anchor a distance medley relay team he was putting together for a meet in Houston. I had always run well in races in Houston. I was so eager to run the relay, I drove the seven hours in a steady downpour to be a part of it. Leonard ran his best mile that year, but he wanted to run the 3/4-mile leg on the relay. I figured he was good for a 2:53 or so on the three-lap leg, as I knew that Roger Bannister had run 2:52.9 in a time trial a year before he broke 4 minutes for the first time. If I ran my best mile on the anchor, I felt our relay team could approach the world record.

As I drove through the rain toward Houston, I hoped that it would be clear, dry, and calm at the meet. It was not. When I arrived it was still raining hard. Water was curb deep on the track, and the wind was blowing 20 to 25 mph. The conditions were hopeless. Splashing through three laps, Leonard ran 3:12, missing the time we hoped for by almost 20 seconds. I concluded my anchor mile with a 26-second 220 downwind, a burst that brought me to the finish in 4:19.9. As soon as I carried the baton across the finish line, the rest of the meet was canceled.

Every serious runner knows that luck is a factor in the pursuit of personal best performances. Variables like the weather, competition, track conditions, and the whims of the human body each have veto power over records, personal and otherwise. Roger Bannister recognized this when he saw the wind conditions at the Iffley Road track on May 6, 1954, the day he was to make his attempt to break 4:00. He thought he might have to postpone the race, which was set up specifically for his record attempt. He hoped the wind would die down. Miraculously, it did.

When I was at OU, several milers planned to run the invitational mile in the John Jacobs Relays to try for Oklahoma's first sub-4 mile. I was in that group, but I knew when I arrived at the track, the race was already a bust. As often occurs during the spring, the wind was roaring at gale force, gusting to 40 miles per hour. We hoped the wind would miraculously diminish. It did not. Though we tried mightily, nature prevailed on that day. Our times were not worth mentioning here.

What Was Happening?

The relay in Houston set the tone for my 1973-74 season. It was a season of confusion. What was happening? By extrapolation, this was supposed to be my year for sub-4. But my performances were dismal. Were they merely a consequence of unfavorable weather? Was this just a brief slump? Had too much anaerobic running put me in decline, or was this a plateau I could work my way out of?

Looking back, I see that I had reached a plateau, a terminal one as it turned out, in the summer of 1972 after I ran an almost effortless 4:02.1 in Houston. A week later in Wichita, I ran a 4:03.9 in the qualifying round of the National Federation Championships. In the final the next day, I ran 4:05.1, though I probably lost 2 seconds in jostling that pushed me off the track. A week later I won two more mile races without serious competition, and another a week later I raced 1,500 meters in 3:45.5 in the National AAU in Seattle in the qualifying round. There I needed to run at least a 41-second last 300 to qualify for the next round but came up with only a 43. I returned to Maryland, where I was on active duty with the Army at Fort Meade, and ran a triple (my first and only) in the Baltimore Municipal Games just two days after the Seattle race. I felt remarkably good in easily winning the mile in

4:08.6 and the 3-mile in 14:22.7, and finishing second in the 880 in 1:53.6 in a span of two hours.

Nine races in four weeks. Too many. My plateau apparently began during this series. I should have paid heed to Arthur Lydiard's warning about running too many anaerobic workouts and too frequent races. At that time, however, my performances were better than ever. But in hind-sight, I believe it was impossible to recognize a plateau in its beginning; such things develop gradually. It is very difficult to do on subtle performance differences of 2 or 3 seconds per mile in a race, differences that cannot be discerned from random ups and downs caused by weather, fatigue, dehydration, and race tactics.

Help From the Log Book

In view of what Lydiard told me, I should have at least studied my running log book and asked myself: had I been racing too much and resting too little?

A runner's log is like the laboratory notebook I learned to use as an engineering student. Every training regimen, indeed every workout is an experiment, and the log book is essentially an experimenter's notebook. In two decades of daily and twice-daily workouts, my entries into my spiral binder logs grew to more than 1,000 pages.

There are several issues for which a detailed logbook is helpful: Am I actually improving? Is my training balanced among aerobic running, anaerobic workouts, racing, and resting? Am I recovering adequately? Do I rest and taper enough for races? Do I allow for enough active rest after each race? Am I properly alternating hard and easy workout days? Am I finishing my workouts feeling exhilarated? Is there inconsistency in races indicating overtraining? Am I due for an active-rest break from running?

The log can serve to answer these questions and help in making adjustments. It should be reviewed often for trends, which seldom become apparent over just a couple of weeks. In 1972, I did not look hard enough into my logbook to ask these questions; nor did I do so in '73, '74, or '75.

I was flat in my performances in 1973 and 1974 while training at 40 to 60 miles per week, but I was running well in longer road races of 10 and 13.1 miles (doing so was poor judgement). In '74, I won an indoor 2-mile in Montgomery, Ala. I then ran a string of six disappointing mile races, interrupted only by a 4:03.8 win at the University of Tennessee. I described that race in Knoxville in my log as one of my best mile races ever, no pain, not tired at the end. But it wasn't a personal best.

As 1975 began, I might have questioned whether there was any problem at all. The indoor season began auspiciously with three run-like-a-deer performances on banked-board tracks indoors. First, I won a 2-mile in Richmond, Virginia, on an 11-lap-to-the mile track in 8:46.0. I noted in my logbook that I ran the first mile in 4:21, feeling like I was merely jogging. Two weeks later I won another 2-mile in Montgomery, Ala., on a 10-lap track, also in 8:46.0 with almost the same splits. This race came 3 hours after I anchored the Atlanta Track Club's distance medley relay to a win over the University of Tennessee with a 4:08.2.

Four weeks later I ran a 13:29.5 in the 3-mile in the National AAU Championships in New York City on the 11-lap Madison Square Garden track. I ran in sixteenth place most of the way with mile splits of 4:26 and 4:32 before finishing tenth. Mirits Yifter of Ethiopia, who would win the 5,000 and 10,000 in the 1980 Olympics, came close to the world indoor record in winning in 13:07.6. I was pleased that after 33 laps of that 160-yard track, Yifter the Shifter did not lap me.

Back to reality, I ran mile races four times in the spring of 1975, each in conditions that could have produced a new personal best. My performance each time was, however, a disappointing 4:05-something.

Then, on the Fourth of July, I returned to the Peachtree 10K in Atlanta. This turned out to be the race that marked the end of my aspirations for a sub-4 mile. I had won this race two years earlier over a relatively small field of 600 runners. This time, the field was twice the size, but I had expectations of winning it again. My right Achilles tendon, which I first injured seven years earlier, was sore from start to finish, and I placed twenty-eighth. At one time or another, I had beaten all but two of the 27 runners who finished ahead of me.

With the plateau confirmed, how could I rise above it? From what I've observed, the typical response among runners is to train harder, to double down on the training that has brought them to a high level of performance. This would mean increasing mileage and/or increasing the intensity of interval training, running more anaerobically. I knew better than to do that, but I did not know what *to* do.

Four years before he broke 4 minutes, Roger Bannister was awarded a research scholarship from Merton College, Oxford. This led to his conducting treadmill tests on athletes, including himself, aimed at better understanding the physiology of exercise. It was painstaking work, which he described as entirely academic, and he felt he did not derive much if any practical benefit from the research. At that time, research in exercise physiology was still in the characterization phase. The practical application to runner training—determining how best to train—would be the goal of later studies by many brilliant scientists. It would be several years, however, before such scientific research would significantly benefit runners' training. Bannister predicted that training would remain empirical for the foreseeable future. Actually, it was the distant future.

With my best performances coming in the mile and 2-mile I, like other middle- and long-distance runners in the 1970s, believed in the primacy of maximal oxygen uptake, better known as VO2max or aerobic capacity. My physiological goal in running 100 miles per week in the off-seasons was to increase my VO2max, though it was a vague goal, having never been measured. Some runners were pushing themselves to crazy levels of over 200 miles per week seeking the same goal without knowing the risk-reward relationship of achieving it.

Perceptions about the singular importance of VO2max began to change in the 1970s when Dr. David Costill published results of treadmill tests on elite marathon runners. He found that although VO2max is central to distance running success, it does not correlate well with marathon performance. He showed that oxygen consumption at a less-than-maximal running speed varied about 15 percent among highly trained runners—and that when runners of equal ability compete, VO2max often fails to predict the winner. His findings indicate that there are two other factors that strongly influence performance—running economy and the ability to run at a high percentage of VO2max without accumulating blood lactate.[53]

In 1971, he published results of tests of Derek Clayton, the Australian who in 1969 set a world record of 2:08:34 for the marathon. Costill measured Clayton's VO2max at 69.7 milliliters of oxygen per kg per minute. Good but not great, his VO2max was lower than that of other elite marathoners. In tests, Clayton was, however, able to run at 86 percent of his VO2max without lactate accumulation for 30 minutes [54], and would likely have been able to maintain this pace for another hour. Most distance runners can perform at 75 to 80 percent of VO2max in the marathon. Costill found that Clayton and other elite marathoners—Bill Rodgers, Frank Shorter, Grete Waitz, and Alberto Salazar—could achieve 85 to 90 percent comfortably.[55]

Costill's work became a model for testing endurance athletes, a triad of tests that gained acceptance internationally in the exercise physiology community in the 1980s. The three parts of the triad are: VO2max, maximal lactate steady state as a percentage of VO2max, and running economy defined as power per oxygen uptake at submaximal speeds.

How does this triad point toward a training change to lift a runner from flat or declining performances? The answer seems apparent in the testing and performance of another marathon world record holder, Paula Radcliffe. Before she ran her first marathon at age 29, Radcliffe was a precocious middle-distance runner who won her first world junior cross-country title at age 17.

Dr. Andrew Jones, a physiologist in the U.K., first tested Radcliffe at age 18, then 11 more times from 1992 to 2003. He found that at age 18, when running less than 30 miles per week, Radcliffe had a remarkably high VO2max of 72 milliliters per kg per minute. Over the next 10 years her VO2max varied around an average of 70, and in 2003 it was the same as it was in 1992.[56] During this period of VO2max plateau, however, she improved steadily from 8:51 to 8:22 in the 3,000 meters, the event she raced almost every year. She ran her first marathon in 2:18:56 in April 2002, then improved to a world women's record of 2:17:18 in the fall of 2002. In the spring of 2003, she ran 2:15:25, the fastest marathon ever run by a woman.

Despite a VO2max Plateau, Paula Radcliffe Set a World Record

How could she improve so much without increasing her VO2max? Jones found that over this period, her running speed at lactate steady state increased by 25 percent, and that her running economy improved by 15 percent. He also reported that her weight training became more sophisticated during the period of study, resulting in improved leg strength and power, as indicated by her vertical leap of 15 inches (38 cm) in 2003, compared to 11.4 inches (29 cm) in 1996. He suggested that strength training and possibly greater flexibility and frequent training at altitude could have improved her running economy. He did not, however, acquire data to support these latter two possibilities.

Though I was no longer competing when these studies were published, I wanted to know what I could have done to lift my performances off the plateau. As estimated with Costill's equations,

[57] my VO2max did not appear to change significantly between 1972 (77.6 calculated for a 4:02 mile) and 1975 (76.6 for an 8:46 two-mile).

Each person has an inherited limit on VO2max. As implied by studies of Paula Radcliffe and Jim Ryun, high responders apparently reach their limit very quickly in their careers, and further training of similar or greater intensity fails to increase VO2max.

In training harder to achieve what may be unachievable, there is a risk of losing strength and power of the legs due to the accumulation of muscle damage, particularly in the more heavily loaded fast-twitch muscle fibers of the lower leg. If weakened by un-repaired damage and unrestored glycogen, the calf muscles can fail to position the Achilles tendon steadfastly with each stride, reducing running economy, as discussed in Chapter 15.

The focus of my training should therefore have shifted toward less frequent interval workouts of similar intensity (performed at the lactate threshold). In a study published in 1981, scientists at the University of Illinois at Chicago found that runners who had increased their VO2max by 20 percent on 10 weeks of six-days-per-week high intensity training could maintain that VO2max on as few as two workouts per week of the same intensity.[58]

I should have also taken a two-month break from running and during this break performed only weight training three days per week to strengthen the legs and hips. Gains in leg and hip strength are likely to support a higher maximal lactate steady state by increasing the quantity of myofibrils generating power for propulsion. This would distribute the workload among more myofibrils. Threshold training to develop more mitochondria, lactate-transport molecules, muscle enzymes, and capillary support in the new myofibrils would facilitate lactate oxidation and/or clearing. Each of the new myofibrils would, of course, include titin strands that would increase the elastic stiffness of the muscles, improving power amplification and energy recycling for improved running economy. I should have rested more each week, increasing my active rest days to two per week.

In 1954, Bannister, Landy, and Santee each had an equal chance at being the first to break 4 minutes. They were apparently equal in talent, and they faced a common challenge: learning how best to train and how often to race. Bannister broke 4:00 first, possibly because of his intuitive approach to training and his understanding of the necessary balance among training, racing, and resting. He was his own coach. Landy too applied the intuitive approach stating, "I am very much a train as you feel man."[59] He broke 4:00 just six weeks after Bannister. Santee, a product of empirical training, never broke 4:00, reaching a best of 4:00.5 in 1955. He might have become the first to run sub-4 were it not for the effects of too frequent racing—too much anaerobic running. He ran out of time, ending his career on a performance plateau with no knowledge of how to rise from it.

This leads to the question of how best to strengthen the legs, which is addressed in the next chapter.

Chapter Seventeen
What I neglected: rebuilding leg and hip strength

Two years before I went out for high school track, I became a weightlifter. I did so with no particular goal in mind, but I knew that strength training could make skinny guys stronger and more muscular. This I knew from Charles Atlas' ads in comic books famously touting transformational benefits for 97-pound weaklings. I was not a 97-pound weakling. At that time, I weighed 145.

I began my transformation after my father, a Prudential Insurance agent, sold a policy to an Army major who was a long-time weightlifter stationed at Fort Sill, the huge artillery post adjacent to Lawton. Fort Sill delivered loud, frequent reminders of its proximity with artillery blasts that rattled dishes in our kitchen cabinets and with cargo helicopters taking off over our neighborhood. They flew so low that our dog Skippy, a dachshund not gifted with great speed, often engaged in a losing race against helicopter shadows moving at high speed down our street when the sun was high.

My Dad asked the major if he would show me and my brothers how to lift weights. I was eager to try. My brothers were not, so I began to train alone. I worked out three times a week on our carport, using a weight set my Dad bought for me. I performed a dozen exercises in each workout, including squats, deadlifts, bench presses, bicep curls, calf raises, and others.

I was motivated by curiosity: will weight-lifting really make me stronger? How long will it take to become much stronger? Will I eventually have a physique like Charles Atlas? I would learn that in weight lifting the answers are revealed quite clearly.

After about a year, I began to see substantial strength gains. Every so often, I posed like Mr. Atlas in front of a mirror, flexing my biceps and pectorals. I measured the circumference of various muscle groups to confirm that weight lifting was indeed making my muscles larger. After two years, I was amazed by my strength gains. The single-repetition maximum I achieved when I weighed 150 pounds was 225 pounds in the bench-press, 325 in the deadlift, 150 in the military press, 190 in the clean and jerk, and 230 in the squat.

There was another effect too, although I don't have before-and-after data to support it. I am certain that the squats, deadlifts, and calf exercises helped me rapidly improve in speed and endurance once I began running the 880 and 440 in track.

In my four-month-long first season of track, my 880-yard run progression went like this: 2:25 in my first race, then 2:10, 2:05, 2:03, and 2:01. My 440 times went from 55.6 in my first time-trial to 51.6 in the 4x440 relay in the conference meet. The improvement did not place me on a watch-list for future Olympians, but no other runner on the Lawton High track team improved as rapidly as I did.

Footraces are contests of power, so powerful legs and hips are valuable attributes for runners. Two good examples of such power are those of world-record holders in the 1960s, Peter Snell and Jim Ryun. Snell's stride was so powerful he was known to scar the tracks on which he ran, kicking up debris with his spikes on cinder or grass tracks. As noted in Chapter 9, Wes Santee observed that Jim Ryun had "the most powerful-looking thighs he had ever seen on a distance runner."

Beyond subjective observations, several scientific studies have shown that strength training improves running economy. A study conducted at the Norwegian University of Science and Technology showed that after eight weeks of strength training, there was a 5 percent improvement in running economy and a 21.3 percent improvement in time to exhaustion at maximal aerobic speed. The study involved 17 well-trained long-distance runners performing four sets of four repetitions of half-squats at maximum weight three times per week. There was no change in maximal oxygen uptake or body weight among the nine male and eight female participants.[60]

The quantity of a person's muscle fibers, the largest and most complex cells of the body, is established at or soon after birth. Muscle fibers do not increase in number, but the myofibrils within them do. Muscles are bundles of bundles of bundles. Each muscle fiber is a bundle of roughly 1,000 to 2,000 myofibrils. Each motor unit in a muscle of the leg contains a bundle of as many as 1,000 muscle fibers; and each muscle contains a bundle of several motor units, each activated electrically by a neuron controlled by the brain.

Strength training stimulates the development of more myofibrils within the muscle fibers, increasing the volume and cross-section area of each muscle. When a myofibril is added, it brings with it titin molecules, the biological springs that protect the myofibril from over-stretching. The titin also amplifies the power. With each new myofibril also come mitochondria, the bacteria-size power plants that convert the stored energy of the fuel and oxygen to kinetic energy; myoglobin for temporary storage of oxygen; lactate transport molecules; capillaries; enzymes for accelerating the reactions in the mitochondria; and storage space for fuel (glycogen granules), all of which can be added with further training.

Each new myofibril is thus a power module that increases a runner's power and helps amplify it. It also improves the energy recycling and running economy. The additional myofibrils also spread the workload among more myofibrils, increasing the ability to sustain power.

The longer the athlete continues weight training two or three times per week the more myofibrils are developed and the stronger and more elastic the muscle becomes. Bill Bowerman once described this process in simple terms in his off-the cuff remarks to incoming freshmen runners at the University of Oregon. [61]

> *"Take a primitive organism, any weak, pitiful organism. Say a freshman. Make it lift or jump or run. Let it rest. What happens? A little miracle. It gets a little better. It gets a little stronger or faster or more enduring. That's all training is. Stress. Recover. Improve. You'd think any damn fool could do it."*

When it comes to weight training to strengthen runners' legs, however, any damn fool apparently cannot do it. What baffles some runners and coaches is the importance of *rest* in the equation.

Developing new myofibrils usually requires at least 48 hours rest between weight workouts for the body to work its little miracles of adaptation. The stimulus for muscle growth is muscle damage, but the damage and recovery period must be controlled so that the myofibril growth is not stunted by too much damage. Strengthening a muscle involves temporarily weakening the muscle by damaging it. Restoration and repair occur during the recovery period.

How Weight Training is Superior For Strength Gains

Precise control of the weight used for each exercise, the rate of increasing the weight over time, and the recovery period make weight training superior to other methods of strength building—such as, hill running, plyometrics, elastic bands, pushing/pulling sleds, running with parachutes, or the quick stop-and-go action of soccer, lacrosse, rugby, tennis, etc. Snell played rugby and tennis before becoming a runner, and that may have helped him develop the power of his legs and hips. These other methods, however, allow for very little control of muscle damage and little certainty that strengthening is actually occurring.

With weight training, control is achieved through timely feedback. If in each succeeding week of weight training, one is able to increase the weight being used with the same number of repetitions, the message is that the training is successful. If there is no progress, the message is to increase the rest to, for example 72 hours. Over a longer term of a month or two, a tape measure can show that a muscle or muscle group has become larger in circumference, proof that myofibrils have been added.

The Problem of Interference

When runners don't see positive results in weight training for the legs, the problem often lies in the rest period, the day of rest after the weight workout. Failing to rest results in what is known as interference. This occurs when a running workout, perhaps an intense one, is performed in the period that should be reserved for rest, preventing full recovery from the weight workout. Recovery involves not only repairing muscle but also restoring glycogen to the muscles.

Progressive overload weight training typically involves high energy expenditure. Three sets of 10 repetitions at the 10-rep maximum can result in depleting about 25 percent of the target muscles' glycogen.[62] Running after a workout of squats, dead lifts, or leg presses can result in a leaden, lifeless feeling of the legs. I learned this by experience in my senior cross-country season at OU when a new coach required our cross-country team to perform weight training, including squats, as part of our morning workouts three days a week. In both the morning and afternoon running workouts, our legs felt dead. We eventually talked the coach out of these weight workouts.

The best way to insert weight training for the legs and hips in a runner training program is to do so in a period between racing seasons, when there are fewer, lighter running workouts or none at all. Elite sprinters do this and gain maximum benefit from the weight training, but most distance runners, particularly high schoolers do not. The reason, it appears, is that distance runners place priority on *running* workouts. In most high school seasons, there are only three or four months in which to work into racing shape then race one or more times per week. It is a scheduling problem. Some coaches require that both strength training for the legs and hips be performed concurrently as a part of the daily workouts.[63] This leads to interference, essentially a mode of overtraining.[64]

An off-season program eliminates interference and allows more time for strengthening to occur. An off-season strengthening program for the legs and hips is what I should have applied in pursuit of a sub-4 mile. Failing to do so was the second most important mistake I made. The over-training and marathoning in the summer of 1968 was the most important mistake.

What I should have done when my mile performances plateaued at age 26 was to take a three-month break from running to focus on progressive overload weight training. This would have involved two or three days of weight training per week and 15 minutes a day of easy active-rest workouts—jogging or walking, that would not engage the fast-twitch muscles—on the days of no weight lifting.

I always felt compelled to run track workouts or distance runs six or seven days a week. I never questioned, except after my racing days had ended, that a running workout was more beneficial than a weight workout or a rest day after a weight workout. I did not know that over time, leg strength can be lost as a result of un-repaired damage to the fast-twitch muscle.

Fast-glycolytic and fast-oxidative-glycolytic muscle fibers are more susceptible to damage than are slow-oxidative muscle fibers. This is probably because their Z-disks are thinner than those of slow-oxidative muscle. The Z-disks are bulkheads spaced every two microns in the myofibrils. Titin springs that protect the myofibrils from overstretching are attached to the Z-disks. Studies have shown that when myofibrils are damaged, the fractures occur around the Z-disks.

Studies have shown too that as people age, their fast-twitch muscle fibers tend to disappear. One study examined the differences in muscle characteristics of older, endurance-trained athletes who had engaged in lifelong regular aerobic exercise compared to younger recreational athletes. The older athletes were found to have significantly fewer and smaller fast-glycolytic muscle fibers and a greater proportion of slow oxidative muscle fibers than the younger athletes.[65]

The fast-twitch are likely to disappear with the stresses of racing, particularly long-distance races, and with occasional killer workouts that require more recovery time than the runner allows. I resumed interval workouts and races quickly after my two very stressful marathons in 1968 and '70. I should have taken it easy for two months afterwards.

Not given time to repair and rebuild, my leg muscles were losing power at an imperceptible rate. I was damaging the myofibrils beyond immediate repair, or eventual repair, and the result was declining performance as the damage became cumulative.

David Costill conducted a study of the vertical leap performance of runners at his Ball State University Human Performance Lab. He found that the group of elite marathoners he tested had a mean vertical leap of only 13.5 inches, compared to an average of 20.9 inches for a group of untrained people. The vertical leap is an indicator of power. He describes the case of Lou Castagnola, a marathoner who had just run his career-best of 2 hours, 17 minutes. Castagnola's vertical leap was only 11.5 inches. Later, he stopped running, and when he was tested again after three years of sedentary life, his vertical leap had improved to 20.3 inches, while his VO2max had decreased by more than a third.

Could this return-of-power effect be what Billy Mills experienced in his remarkable comeback after 1 ½ years of no training before he won the Olympic gold medal in 1964 in the 10,000 meters?

Weight training offers two important bonuses. Studies based on echocardiograms indicate that weight-lifting strengthens the heart by thickening the muscles that form the walls of the heart. Weight-lifting also increases the secretion of testosterone and growth hormones.[67]

Weight lifting for the legs and hips is a win, win, win situation of which neither I nor most middle-and long-distance runners have taken full advantage.

Chapter Eighteen
Catch-as-catch-can training and road racing

Perhaps the most influential runner I never met but came to know was Fred Wilt. He was not a coach but a runner who would never have become a two-time Olympian if not for his strong resolve and desire to learn the science of runner training. He began, as I did, with no apparent talent for running.

I got to know Fred through correspondence. I helped him compile data from runners around the world for his three-volume set of *How They Train*. The best, most encouraging story in his books is how he himself developed into a world-class runner.[68]

When Fred went out for track as a freshman at a small Indiana high school in 1935, he showed no potential for future greatness. He was the only member of the track team who wanted to be a miler, but he had no background in athletics, and neither he nor his coach knew anything about runner training. He would run two or three times a week, covering two miles at a slow pace each time, believing that if he could endure two miles in training, one mile in a race would be easy. He soon realized this was a flawed approach.

"Each race was a bitter experience in terms of exhaustion, and I suffered many infuriating defeats," he explained years later. His singular strength was his motivation to excel, but failure was the inevitable result of his efforts, as it would be for any newcomer lacking coaching, knowledge of training, or signs of natural talent for running. The odds weighed heavily against his success as a runner; he probably should have tried tennis or baseball. But he stuck with running.

It would be five years before he began to see significant improvement. That's when he enrolled in Indiana University and began to train under its distinguished track coach, Earle C. "Billy" Hayes, who was then the most successful middle-distance coach in the U.S. Hayes, who coached the 1936 U.S. Olympic team, introduced Fred to a novel training method that had emerged from Europe—interval training. In the first two months he was coached by Hayes, Fred improved his two-mile time from 10:10 to 9:22.

"Racing, which had before meant only pain and exhaustion, now provided me with a feeling of joy in conquering personal fatigue. Hayes taught me the what, how, and why of training as he knew it," he explained in *How They Train*. Hayes was not just a coach but a teacher of training and racing. From Hayes, Fred learned how to be his own coach.

At Indiana University, Fred won two NCAA championships, one in cross-country and one in the 2-mile run in track. After graduation, he coached himself and continued to improve, winning eight national AAU titles, setting five American records from 2 miles to 10,000 meters, competing in two Olympic Games, and winning the Sullivan Award given annually to the outstanding amateur athlete in the U.S. He became a career FBI agent and continued to train and race until he was 35 years old.

I learned much from Fred Wilt, both from the example he set in coaching himself and what he described as a *catch-as-catch-can* training, working out early in the morning and late at night to accommodate the demands of a family and full-time job. Catch-as-catch-can is a term from old style wrestling that means "when opportunity presents itself." For runners, it means that there is very little time available to train on a regular schedule. The part of the healthy triad that is typically most neglected is sleep. This was the period in which demands of my job, being a husband and father to three young children, traveling for work, and community involvement made it difficult to optimize my training.

A Path Similar to Fred Wilt's

My path in running was similar to Fred's. I had learned very little about training in my one season of high school track, but I learned much with J.D. Martin's coaching at OU. After college I continued to improve for two years being self-coached, but I saw my performances plateau at age 27, though I was not ready to consider retiring.

I moved from Texas to Maryland in the spring of 1974 to begin working as civilian engineer for the U.S. Army at Edgewood Arsenal. I found the Arsenal to be an ideal place to train after work on its quiet roads. I also trained often on one of the high school tracks in the town of Bel Air 10 miles away.

I trained with less intensity than I had in previous years. I found a good balance between workouts and rest that enabled me to win most of the races I entered in the Baltimore region. For the first time since leaving college I became a part of a running community, a close knit supportive one in Harford County, Maryland. After three years of running solo, I had several runners to train with, and we helped each other. I won scores of local races. If foot-racing is an act of ego, becoming part of the Harford County running community was an ego-booster.

In my 28 years working at Edgewood, I continued training daily except for a six-month stretch in 1987 after breaking my leg. I often worked out twice a day, even when traveling as required by the job. I became adept at catch-as-catch-can training, seldom missing a day's workout when traveling across the U.S. or to Canada, England, Norway, South Korea, Saudi Arabia, Kuwait, United Arab Emirates, and El Salvador.

Strange Experiences in Training

Having run as long and often as I did, I accumulated some unique experiences, some good, some bad. Once, on a 4-mile run before dawn in Western Massachusetts, I slipped on an ice patch and scraped my knee in 14-below-zero cold; the blood froze on my sweatpants. On a long run in Ohio, I got lost, ran 12 miles instead of 6, and finished in a snow shower after darkness fell. One night, I was hit by a half empty beer can thrown from a car. Another time I was shot in the back with a BB gun from a passing car on a quiet road. I ran the small perimeter path at bombed-out Ali Al Salem Air Base in Kuwait just 23 miles from Iraq after the first gulf war, advised to be very careful in doing so. In the capital of El Salvador, I was told I could be killed or kidnapped if I ran through the city. I opted to run on the hotel treadmill.

An owl once delivered a blow to the top of my head as I ran one night in Bel Air. This was when I had begun to lose my hair, and the moonlight reflecting off my bald spot might have caught its attention. His touch-and-go maneuver caught *my* attention. Owls' wings do indeed produce silent flight. After that, I began wearing a baseball hat to protect from the unlikely occurrence of a second owl attack.

I was present, though not competing, when a bizarre tragedy occurred during a marathon at Edgewood Arsenal in 1987. Midway through the annual Last Train to Boston Marathon, a single-engine airplane crashed on the course about 50 meters in front of the lead runner. The pilot had taken off with one passenger aboard from the post airfield minutes earlier when the engine failed. Attempting to glide to a safe landing on the paved road on which the marathoners were running, the pilot allowed the plane to stall, a fatal mistake that caused it to plummet. It banked sharply out of control near the ground and crashed wing-down in flames. Both the pilot and passenger died in the crash. It was gliding silently, like an owl, when it approached the lead runner from behind before turning in front of him. Stunned, he was unable to render any aid or to continue running. He abandoned the race, as did all the other runners behind him.

Catch-as-catch-can training served me well, allowing me to continue my pursuit of the sub-4 mile for two more years. I ran well in longer track races indoors in 1974 and '75. But four disappointing mile races in 1975 in ideal conditions seemed to indicate I had reached a performance plateau, one that was apparently going to last. My final run-like-a-deer race in the mile occurred just before my twenty-seventh birthday on the University of Tennessee track in May of 1974. I won the race in 4:03.82 after taking the lead with a half-lap to go. My kick felt strong but produced only a 28-second last 220. Had I started kicking earlier I might have run a personal best. I rated how I felt as a 9 on a scale of 10, and I described the race in my logbook as one of the best mile races ever, no pain, not tired at the end, good kick last 70 yards. But I did not have the same zip I had two years earlier.

The Logical Next Step: Road Racing

Turning to road racing was a logical next step for me at age 29. I searched for my niche, my best racing distance if it wasn't to be the mile. Many runners do this after competing in high school or college track and cross-country. They think the marathon holds the most potential for success. It requires less power, but it requires more resilience and durability.

I was not interested in returning to the marathon. I began to run more road races ranging from 3 miles to the half marathon. I no longer had specific goals in running, but I had plenty of inertia. Inertia is the tendency of an object at rest to remain at rest, and an object in motion to remain in motion. The former is couch-potato inertia; the latter was, of course, my running inertia. Running had become an engrained habit, and I continued workouts, mostly twice a day throughout this road-racing phase, which lasted 10 years from 1976 until an abrupt ending on January 22, 1987.

What was attractive about road racing? Road races are more abundantly available, and have a much friendlier culture. Every runner in a race is given his or her finishing time, and all runners are eligible for age-group awards. The competitors double as spectators and fans; they run along back in the pack, cheering the lead runners at the turnaround, finish, and awards presentation. In October 1981, on my second date with a young Baltimore woman named Joann Kolarik, we ran the 8-mile Baltimore Subway road race. I finished fourth, and she, 1004th. I won an age-group award. She won my heart. Eight months later we were married.

For a miler, an additional advantage is that the race pace is slower, so a longer race doesn't require as much aerobic power to compete well. With the running economy milers possess, they are able to apply less power, e.g. 80 percent power, when running at a good pace in the longer races. Both power and economy tend to peak and decline in runners after a certain age or a certain number of years of hard training and racing, but this age of decline usually comes later in life.

I ran my first road race in the 1968 Richardson Road Race in Texas. I was encouraged to do so by reading a magazine article about all the prizes that were presented at New England road races. At Richardson that year, there were no prizes, just trophies, and I didn't win one. The Bel Air Town Run 5K, which I won three times, had lots of prizes each year, including bicycle each year, but they were awarded by random drawing, and I never won anything beyond trophies.

In 1972, I ran well in road races such as the Cade's Cove 10-miler in Tennessee, the Stone Mountain 10-miler in Georgia, the White Rock Lake 11-miler in Dallas, the Gunpowder Neck 10-miler in Maryland. I won all of these, which was encouraging, but I know now that they were pushing my goal of a sub-4 mile further away. These long races weren't as debilitating as marathons, but the time needed for recovery was long.

A Motorcycle Appears. A Sailboat Disappears

In one memorable race in October 1974, I was in contention for a large and unusual prize—a small sailboat—in the Forest Festival Half Marathon in Perry, Florida. The race drew a strong field and the pace was fast despite the sunny, 82-degree weather. I can't say that the prize gave me extra incentive, but I ran my fastest six-mile split, 29:41, in the race. I was in second place through 11 miles, trailing only Neil Cusack, an Olympian, NCAA champion, and Boston Marathon winner from Ireland. Holding a big lead, Neil took a wrong turn near the 3-mile point. I did also but corrected my course more quickly than Neil, losing only about 15 seconds.

I did not see Neil again until a motorcycle passed me 15 minutes later, going about 30 miles per hour. The passenger on the back did not wave or smile, but I could see it was Neil. The race director apparently recognized that the turn at which he and I went astray was poorly marked, and that turning Neil's race temporarily into a motorized biathlon would be only fair for this distinguished runner who was sure to win easily absent the wrong turn. Once the motorcycle returned Neil to his approximate position in the lead, I remained in second place until the heat got to me at 9 ½ miles, and slowed my pace to 5:40-per-mile. Jeff Galloway passed me at 11 miles and Marty Liquori at 12. When I could not hold off either of them, I saw in my mind the sailboat drifting out to sea. Cusack finished first in 1:05:11 and, as expected, was disqualified for his motorcycle assistance. Galloway won the sailboat in 1:07:32, and I finished fourth in 1:08:30, 15 seconds behind Liquori. I didn't need a boat anyway.

Nevertheless, having found that I could do well at longer distances, I was hooked on road racing, although I should have waited until my mile-running days were behind me.

I had adapted well with catch-as-catch-can training and continued it for a decade. I believe now that my decline in performance over that period was due in part to the chronic injury to my Achilles tendons. Tendons don't heal the same way muscles do; tendons heal as if a dab of glue is applied across many broken collagen fibers, which means they do not return to their original elastic stiffness. Consequently, my biological springs were no longer well-tuned to amplify maximum power generated by the muscles of the upper legs. I also believe my leg strength was diminished, as I had never taken the time to restrengthen the legs with progressive overload weight training. That includes the calf muscles, which are the most heavily abused in racing. The gastrocnemius is about half fast-twitch muscle, which is not as durable as the slow twitch, and my calf muscles could no longer rigidly hold the proper foot angle at a pace of 4 minutes per mile. They probably could do quite well at 5 minutes per mile, at which the force on the legs upon landing is much less.

A Final Hot-Weather Marathon

Road racing eventually drew me back to the marathon, even though my Achilles tendons had not healed. In 1977, I ran my third and fourth marathons, the fourth being the Boston Marathon on a hot Patriots' Day in mid-April. It was sure to be another battle against heat injury, and if this battle turned out to be worse than what I endured in my first two marathons, there would be no more. I resolved to drink as often as practical during the race.

My goal at Boston was ambitious, to better 2 hours, 20 minutes, which meant averaging 5:20 per mile. When I saw that the race day would be hot a one, I did not change my goal, but I changed my socks just before the start. That meant sitting on the ground amid a forest of 6,000 legs. It was a weird ambience for a footwear adjustment, which did not have the beneficial effect I anticipated. My feet began to burn just 3 miles into the race.

I maintained a 5:20 per mile pace past Wellesley College, the half way point, but as I crested a hill at about 16 miles, I could see the Prudential Center in the distance, its image distorted by rising heat currents, not unlike what I remembered from the movie *Lawrence of Arabia*. It appeared to be 100 miles away. I felt that I had to end my race, terminate the revival of my ill-fated marathoning career, and never again run a long race in the heat. I glanced at my watch—it was just past 1 p.m.—and looked around for a way to get off the course and perhaps find a taxi that would transport me to the train station where I could catch my scheduled 4 o'clock Amtrak train back to Maryland.

A simple walk-off exit, however, seemed impossible. The crowd at this point was probably five rows deep on both sides of the road. I could not envision myself walking into the crowd with my arms stretched forward in a V like a New England snow plow, saying, "excuse me, excuse me. I am quitting the race." So, I didn't quit. I reasoned that the quickest way to the train station would be to keep running, even at a slower pace, and that's what I did. I had held my 5:20-per-mile pace through 16 miles, but cramping in my calves, the arch of my right foot, and my diaphragm slowed me over the last 10 miles. I stopped for 30 seconds to adjust my socks and shoes, my new Nike Jayhawks, which I thought would serve me well but were inadequate to mitigate the effects of the hot the pavement. I ran my last six miles at 7 minutes per mile and finished in 2:35:22. The ordeal ended on a positive note: I managed to catch the 4 o'clock train back to Maryland.

My road-racing phase ended on January 22, 1987, it was an unplanned ending, as the next chapter explains.

Chapter Nineteen

No immunity from bad luck

Bad luck, I believe, occurs when two or more unlikely or unexpected events or conditions coincide in such a way that an even less likely misfortune occurs. This can be visualized as the reels of a slot machine, which can stop spinning with an alignment of cherries (good result) or dissimilar symbols (bad result). The randomness of unfortunate alignment can lead to a minor accident, a major one, or a tragedy, depending upon how much kinetic and potential energy is involved.

In 22 years of serious running, I had logged about 40,000 miles on the run, a good portion of it in a variety of unfamiliar places, including a few foreign countries, some of it at night. I was always aware that while running alone, some unlikely coincidence could result in injury, the end of my running career, or worse.

On the mild end of the spectrum of misfortune was my encounter with an unexpected shadowy figure one morning before dawn on the OU golf course. I was cruising comfortably along at 7 minutes a mile when I saw something in my path. It was not until I was perhaps five feet away from it and still at cruise speed that I realized it was a black, furry animal. I then recognized it by both sight and smell. Skunk! When it flipped its tail toward the dark sky, I recognized it to be a threat equivalent to a grenade with its pin already pulled. Skunks don't belong on golf courses, and runners don't either for that matter, particularly in the hours of darkness. But there we were, in an intimate meeting, each experiencing a burst of fear.

Our orientation was less threatening than eye-to-tail, but it still required quick action to avert a crisis of personal hygiene. I needed to backpedal at least 15 meters, like a football cornerback, which I very briefly was in high school. The skunk needed to spin 180 degrees to aim its most pungent and persistent of natural odorants. I moved at great speed and kept going, realizing that I would have to withdraw from classes and all forms of social contact for a week or more if the spray was on target. I knew this from experience. Our dachshund years earlier had a learning experience with a skunk. A fine house pet, he became a yard pet after skunk oil aerosol settled on his body. Luckily, none settled on me.

I often ran on golf courses in college. They were excellent venues for cross-country races, and safe places for training runs, so I assumed. The soft, lush grass of the fairways, however, was not without hazards.

Once on a daylight run on the OU golf course, I found a old piece of broken pottery partially hidden in the rough. I found it with the sole of my foot. A triangular shaped shard found its way into my foot and broke off as it reached a depth of three-quarters of an inch—right through the thin sole of my Tiger racing flats. I was more than a mile away from my dorm, so I had to extract it myself and walk on my heel slowly back to the dorm for first aid. The wound healed fairly quickly, to my surprise.

Another incident occurred on a golf course in Manhattan, Kansas, in my senior year. Warming up for a cross-country dual meet against Kansas State, a teammate and I were stretching in the middle of a fairway. I looked to my right and saw golfers about 100 meters away preparing to tee off. We'd better get off the fairway, I said, and we moved over into the rough, near the trees and resumed our stretching. One golfer proceeded with his tee shot, which flew straight and true, not down the fairway, but towards me. I did not see the ball in flight, however, because I was bending over in a hamstring-stretch ritual, facing away from the tee. My buttocks must have appeared like the "hit it here" sign on the centerfield fence at a baseball game. The ball flew like a heat-seeking missile toward its randomly selected target. If a 150-mph golf ball is to transfer its kinetic energy to the human body, there is no better location for doing so than the buttocks. It struck me on the right buttock, causing more surprise than pain, but as I later noted, just three inches to the left and it would have been a hole in one. I went on to run a good race that morning, placing second, 3 seconds behind Kansas State's best runner, Jerome Howe.

There were other frightful incidents on the run, most of them at night, like the time I ran under a wide road sign that had a 5 foot, 8 inch clearance. I know that to be the clearance because the sign left an impression in my forehead 2 inches down from the top of my head. My body rotated backwards with my forehead being the pivot point, and I landed on my back. I had astutely worn a baseball cap with the bill pulled low to block the light from headlights of oncoming cars. I did not foresee, however, its effect on seeing low-hanging road signs. So much for preparedness.

Fresh, Light Snow Over Ice: Almost Frictionless

My most unfortunate incident on the run occurred years later, also in darkness, not on a golf course but in a church parking lot. The conditions that morning, light snow and scattered, small patches of ice were appropriate only for streakers, runners who take obsession for daily running to the highest level.

I have known several distinguished streakers. Bob Ray, a long-time friend who lives in Baltimore, once had the longest recognized running streak in the U.S. He ran four or more miles every day without missing a day for 38 years. After 100,000 miles on the run, he ended his streak in 2005 on his sixty-eighth birthday without coercion of injury or frailty. Bob was a postman, so he knew a thing or two about the swift completion of appointed rounds despite rain or heat or gloom of night —or snow and ice—but he certainly didn't need supplemental exercise afoot. He was simply in the thrall of an addiction to running.

I admired Bob's assiduity, but I never considered building my own streak. An elite runner, which I aspired to be, does not cultivate streaks but recognizes the importance of rest days and the potential hazards of not taking them. I was, however, driven by habit and a strong desire to carry out every workout *as planned*. My unquantified streak of completing planned workouts ended on January 22, 1987.

My 4-mile run began at 6:30 a.m. as I walked down our driveway and saw snowflakes beginning to fall. I carried in my hand a letter containing a bill payment, which I would deliver on the run to the post-office on Bel Air's Main Street two miles away. (Postman Bob Ray would have been proud.) There was barely a trace of snow on the ground, so the footing was perfect.

On the way back, I cut through a church parking lot a half mile from home, as I often did on my morning runs. By then, the ground was covered by a layer of snow that seemed innocuously thin. There were small islands in the hard-surface parking lot, and my path could have taken me to the right or the left of the first island I approached.

In the pre-dawn darkness that morning, there happened to be a small frozen puddle in the path I randomly took as I neared the island and prepared to veer to the left of it. The patch of ice was smooth and hidden by snow, and in turning I happened to plant my left foot precisely on the hidden ice so that it would slide about 18 inches before reaching firm traction at the edge of the ice. Unfortunately, my lean to the left ensured maximum sliding speed and maximum force upon stopping. All the elements of misfortune were aligned. Whoosh.

Two Audible Snaps

My foot slid, then stopped instantly when it reached the ice-free pavement beneath the snow. The abrupt stop produced a powerful torque, fracturing my tibia with two audible snaps and sending me to the ground. A wave of nausea informed me that I had broken a bone. This, I later reasoned, is how someone breaks a leg slipping on an errant grape while walking around a salad bar. It's not the impact of the fall. It's the torque in the slip and sudden stop. Falling produces secondary damage.

It was still dark, and I was a half mile from home. I saw a figure in the darkness, slowly jogging about 50 yards away. I yelled. It was an acquaintance from the neighborhood, Roy Bulger, with his dog. Just as Roy reached me, a vanpool pulled into the parking lot, stopped nearby, and opened its sliding door. Roy helped me rise and hobble toward the van's open door. Then I addressed the driver, emphasizing with 17 carefully chosen words what I needed to say: "I have broken my leg. I live just a half mile away. Can you take me home?"

The driver took no time at all to consider my request and responded in a formal manner as if I were attempting to sell him a lifetime subscription to *Field and Stream* magazine, in which he had no interest: "I'm sorry we have a carpool to pick up and take to Washington." With that, I laid myself down in the snow, perhaps 10 feet away from the van's open door and began collecting a coating of snowflakes in the darkness. As other members of the carpool arrived, they looked at me, looked away, and entered the van. They soon closed the door and departed without offering even a goodbye, best wishes, or a "hope you get home somehow."

Roy had decided to run to his home about a mile away, leaving me alone for what must have been a half hour (neither he nor his dog were swift afoot). This was before cell phones became commonplace. He returned with his car and transported me to my home. My wife Joann knew something was wrong; I was missing when my own carpool to work came and went. I laid on the living room floor groaning in pain until she drove me to the hospital. In surgery, the fibula was first cut to give access to the tibia, then screws were inserted in the tibia and a rod into the fibula.

Except for two forgettable attempts, I never returned to racing even though I turned 40 six months later, becoming eligible for masters competition.

I should have skipped that early morning workout. The obsession for running that had given me consistency of training for 22 years led me to the end of my racing career.

Falls Have Been Career Enders

Falls have been significant in the careers of other runners. At least three of America's greatest track stars suffered falls that brought each of their careers to a sad end: Jim Ryun fell in the quarterfinals of the 1972 Olympic 1500, ending his comeback. Mary Decker Slaney fell in the 3,000 in the 1984 Olympics, ending her best opportunity to win Olympic gold. Cliff Cushman, a silver medalist in the 400 hurdles in the 1960 Olympics, was likely to win the event in the '64 Olympics, but he fell at the fifth hurdle in the Olympic trials and did not make the team. These falls were witnessed by tens of thousands.

Mine was a quiet fall witnessed by no one, which begs the question: If a runner falls in the darkness, and there is no one around to hear the bone snap, does he make a mournful sound? I did not. The fall did not end my dream of running a sub-4 mile. That dream ended years earlier with the delayed effects of the summer workouts in which I routinely and naively abused my Achilles tendons. When I slipped and fell onto the ice, I was simply stunned. It took me a while to sort out my feelings and address many questions. The main question that came to mind as I lay in the snow was: how long would it be until I could run again?

It took seven months of rehab to be able to able to start jogging again, and even then only twice a week. After nine months, I was able to run what I would call an easy interval workout that was no longer easy, 4 x 400 in 1:35 to 1:45 with 90 seconds rest. During that period of no running followed by lighter running, my weight topped out at 185 pounds, about 30 over my college running weight. Ultimately, however, the broken leg was beneficial in a way: it pulled me back from the training, which by inertia was over-training relative to what I needed to be running as I approached age 40. I needed to heed the advice of Dr. Kenneth Cooper, author of *Aerobics*, and to adhere more closely to the healthy triad.

Chapter Twenty
Venous valves and booster pumps

My accident on the ice set me back more than I expected. Once the fractured tibia healed, the screws were removed, and the rod was taken out of the fibula, I experienced an unlikely reversal of injuries. As one chronic injury began to heal, another injury became chronic. In the three months I was idled for the broken leg, the soreness in my Achilles tendons finally went away. But there remained a persistent pain in the arch of my left foot. I assumed that the powerful torque that broke the tibia also damaged a muscle, tendon or ligament, and that it would eventually heal. I was wrong. The pain and stiffness caused me to limp upon arising each morning, in warming up to run, and in getting up to walk after sitting for more than a few minutes. This remained barely tolerable and lasted *for 33 years*. The total duration of these successive injuries—to the Achilles tendons and then to the left tibia—was *52 years*, surely some sort of unofficial record among runners. What was I thinking? Why did I tolerate the nagging pain for a half century? Because I was a typical runner.

I could not bear to be idle for the long period that would have been required to heal. I rationalized that: (1) in time, the body heals itself; surgery or drugs consequently wouldn't be necessary; (2) therapies such as hot whirlpool baths don't seem to help as much as exercising the injury, and (3) pain killers don't heal and can sometimes slow the healing.

I was wrong. The most effective treatment requires a period of resting the injury completely, even though we serious runners cannot tolerate extended rest. I never wanted to take time off for the Achilles tendons I injured 19 years earlier, and I did not want to submit to surgery on my foot, which would have meant substantial time off. I lacked knowledge about de-conditioning, so I had no confidence in coming back from an extended rest.

Learning About Venous Valves and Muscle Pumps

Later I learned about the tiny valves in the veins of the legs that are essential for running. I didn't know about the role they played in the healing of the foot injury—and in preventing the healing. The following information about valves and pumps may seem trivial, but these obscure little flappers are very important.

Called venous valves, they ensure one-way flow (upward, toward the heart) and operate on free energy from the muscles that power the run. The valves prevent blood from flowing in reverse, which can result in blood pooling in the veins of the feet and legs, leading to damage of the veins. It is my perception that most runners are not familiar with the valves and their function. I knew nothing about them until I was 73.

Then, serendipity. While reading some research about venous valves and muscle pumps, I found a simple home remedy for my chronic injury: I needed to use my muscles pumps properly. Here is what I learned.

Muscle pumps and the venous valves that form them are the auxiliary pumps that assist in lifting the blood from the feet to the heart. They are exquisitely simple, consisting of one-way valves in the veins—not the arteries—of the legs (also the arms and the jaw), and they operate only when the muscles surrounding the veins are active. As these muscles contract, they squeeze the veins, which have thinner, more flexible walls than arteries, causing the blood to flow through them upward if they are working properly. The more frequently the leg muscles contract and relax, the greater is the flow of blood they pump. When these pumps are not active, however, there is little or no return of blood from the feet to the heart. In standing still, the pressure in the veins at the calf muscle is only about 20mm of mercury, not enough to force the blood upward. In running, the muscle pumps increase this pressure to about 90mm.

The upward journey of the blood begins with the foot compressing the veins in the sole. The blood rises in stages with the rhythmic contractions of the muscles through what is usually two valves in each lower leg and two in each upper leg. It then passes through the thorax where pressure changes caused by the action of the lungs give it a boost. Some people have fewer venous valves than normal. Some have none at all, which is a serious handicap for a runner. The valves are almost imperceptible by sight or touch. Only in their absence or their malfunctioning is a runner aware of them.

Their pumping power and the flow rate they produce are substantial. In running, the muscle pumps of the legs are estimated to furnish up to 30 percent of the total power needed to circulate the blood—about 18 percent from the pumps of the thigh muscles and 12 percent from those of the calf muscles. This results in an estimated 20 liters per minute blood flow through the legs while running versus less than 1 liter per minute at rest.[69]

In walking at 100 steps per minute, the calf muscle pumps on both legs combine for a flow rate of about 6 liters per minute. The muscles of the lower legs provide most of this pumping power, with an ejection fraction of about 65 percent.[70]

The Challenge: Keep the Muscle Pumps Working

Problems arise when runners allow the muscle pumps to stop working while the heart continues to pump blood at an elevated flow rate and pressure. This is the scenario when a runner simply stops, stands still, or sits down at the end of a workout or race or during the rest periods among repetitions. This causes blood to pool in the feet and ankles, expanding the flexible veins in the feet and lower legs, creating reservoirs that are detrimental to circulation. It also causes blood to back up in the arteries, like water backing up in sink drain from a clog deep in the drain pipe. As the blood backs up, leakage out of the capillaries can occur, causing it to collect in interstitial spaces among the muscles, bones, and tendons of the feet. This not only inhibits circulation of oxygen and nutrients to the feet; it also takes blood out of circulation, reducing the heart's power and stroke volume, and consequently reducing the supply of blood to the muscles of the heart, brain, and other organs.

Immediate Cool-Down Is Essential

The sudden halt to blood flow through deep veins has been known to cause such a rapid decrease in blood pressure and flow that a runner can faint, particularly after a race and/or in hot weather when blood flow is diverted to the skin through vessels that are dilated.[71]

The simple and effective measure to prevent this from occurring is a proper cool-down. In the 33 years of running after I broke my leg, I always neglected the cool-down. On completing interval workouts (for example, 8 x 2-minute runs with 2-minute rest after each) on the treadmill, I would simply sit down and begin working at the computer even though my pulse was around 150 to 160 beats per minute. As a result, fluid collected in the veins, tissues and cavities of my left foot and ankle, which I had injured years earlier.

The key word is immediate. I learned that I should have kept moving *without delay* after every run that elevated my pulse rate. Even before my accident on the ice, I usually just stood still or ambled a few steps between repetitions of an interval workout on the outdoor track and at the end of every continuous run. In my first 10 years of running, sometimes I jogged between repetitions of an interval workout but I preferred not to. Perhaps this is also the reason my Achilles tendon soreness persisted for 19 years.

Once I learned the importance of the immediate cool down, I began doing a six-minute cool-down, jogging half and walking half, starting immediately at the end of each workout. Jogging, even as slow as 3 mph, provides more pumping action than walking because the cadence of jogging is about twice as fast as that of walking. I also did a similar jog-walk in the two-minute rest period of my interval workouts. In just two weeks of doing this, the arch pain that had persisted for 33 years went away and did not return. It was a miracle cure.

I had also seen evidence that this pooling of blood in the veins can cause a column of blood to build up in the arteries of the legs, affecting the circulation to the both legs when sitting for long periods. This seems to explain how sitting for long periods at the computer without taking a break at least every hour caused the legs to be almost unresponsive in trying to move after getting out of my chair.

Sitting for long periods before a race can present one of the more difficult scenarios for warming up. Riding in a car for an hour or more and arriving shortly before the race is to begin can create the same effect. This requires a longer warmup period, preferably starting with 10 minutes of walking then advancing to jogging and striding to pump the blood from the feet. This restores full circulation to the legs and feet.

Carrying the arms low (extended) in running allows blood to accumulate in the veins of the arms, taking a small amount of blood out of circulation. This effect can be seen in swelling of the fingers when walking, and this is why the arms are carried high, with a bend of about 90-degrees in running. There are venous valves in the arms too, but these are not activated in running unless there is contracting and relaxing of the muscles of the forearms by squeezing and opening the fist in rhythm with running.

Having finally learned about venous valves, muscle pumps, and the scientific basis for cool downs, I gained relief from years of a morning limp and soreness. I then began to wonder if I could make a comeback to compete in the over-70 age group.

First, however, I had to deal with what had become obvious in the years since the fall on the ice—my body was in natural decline. In this period, other problems emerged: fat pads had vanished from the soles of my feet, I developed a case of peripheral neuropathy, and I had lost most of the spring in my stride.

Chapter Twenty-One
Fear of death on the run

There has been a memorial run held annually for several years in Bel Air, Maryland, honoring Scott Dana Smith, a good friend of mine who was a well-known runner locally, a popular grade-school teacher, and a mentor to many runners. Scott was a marathoner. He had completed 34 marathons before he experienced a life-changing event while running a 5-mile road race in March 2010.

Halfway through the race, Scott suddenly felt breathless. In his 30 years of running, he had never failed to finish a race, but this sudden distress alarmed him. He stopped running and walked to the finish line. In the emergency room later, he learned that he had suffered a heart attack. A blood clot had lodged in an artery serving his heart, causing damage to a portion of his heart muscle. In essence, the damage reduced the maximum pumping power his heart could produce. The loss was irreversible, and unless he moderated his running, he was a candidate for another, more serious heart attack.

This seemed an unlikely result of his many years of running, which began on the Bel Air High School track team. He had not missed a day of training in 12 years and was running an average of 50 to 60 miles per week. He felt he was in perfect condition when he began the 5-mile race, just a day after an 18-mile training run in preparation for the Boston Marathon.

Scott remained hospitalized for a week. His level of fitness and self-awareness saved him from a far worse outcome and helped him resume exercising after two months of rehab. First, he began walking, then a month later he ran an easy 5K. Eight months after his heart attack, he completed a marathon, the first of 11 he would run *after* the heart attack. He also ran 19 half marathons. "I still race a lot, but I don't do it as competitively," he told me. "I don't take things for granted like I used to."

Five years later, Scott had a second heart attack, this time in his sleep the night after a routine training run. This one was fatal. He was 46 years old.

Scott was not my first friend to suffer heart failure during or after a run. Over the years, there were several other runners in Bel Air and Harford County whom I knew and wrote about in a weekly runners' column for the county newspaper, *The Aegis*.

Heart Attacks Struck Down Other Runners in My Community

Two years before Scott died, Dr. Tom Jordan finished a workout on the recreation trail in Bel Air and got into his car to leave. He died before he could leave the parking lot. The chief of surgery at the local hospital, he once performed skin cancer surgery on my forearms. During the procedure, he and I conversed constantly about running and runners. He looked perfectly fit and healthy before his sudden death at age 54.

My friend Rob March had decided to skip his workout the day he died. He wasn't feeling well after running 13 miles the day before. Rob was a youthful, enthusiastic athlete who had logged more than 50,000 miles in 21 years of running. A year earlier, while wearing a heart monitor, he found that his heart rate would accelerate rapidly a few miles into a run. This induced him to submit to a treadmill stress test and a month later, catheterization to correct the cause of his irregular heartbeat. His doctors felt confident in the success of the procedure and placed no restrictions on his running. He died in his sleep the night after he skipped his workout. He was 43, the same age at which his father died of a heart attack.

Bill Barnholth came home after a jogging workout, laid down on the couch to take a nap before supper and never awakened. He was 57. A former college football linebacker and power lifter, he had slimmed down from 255 to 180. For 15 years, he was a back-of-the-pack participant in scores of running events, never winning an award but always finishing the race. In the months before he died, he lost 25 pounds by dieting and running 25 miles per week.

Doug Anderson was a state champion runner when he was in high school. In the 15 years after high school, he gained a large amount of weight, topping out at almost 300 pounds before he made a remarkable comeback. Running again, he slimmed down to 195 pounds. At age 37, he finished a mile race in 5 minutes, 15 seconds, and soon after crossing the finish line, he collapsed and died. He had recently undergone a routine physical examination.

Paul Perkovich, the athletic director at C. Milton Wright High School in Bel Air, ran the first of his 15 marathons in 2003 in 5 1/2 hours. He then improved steadily to a personal best of 3:25:10 four years later. He ran the Boston Marathon three times, in 2010, '11, and '12. The fastest time of the three, 3:41:49, came at age 47 in the brutal conditions of 2012—a sunny day in which the temperature rose to 87 degrees. It was one of the hottest Boston Marathons on record. Six and a half years later, he was training for another marathon when he went for a routine run alone one September morning. He did not return. He was 53 years old.

I lost another long-time friend, Dave Starnes, to a heart attack at age 73 after he finished a walking workout. Dave won the North Carolina state high school championship in cross-country in 1962 and '63 and in track in 1964. He developed into a record-setting runner at the University of Maryland, twice winning the Atlantic Coast Conference Championship in the 2-mile run, setting a school record of 8:55. He also set the 3-mile run record of 13:50. Always active, he maintained his slim physique of a distance runner even after knee replacement surgery ended his running, and he turned to hiking, biking, and golfing. It is uncertain, but the artificial knees could have caused a thrombosis that traveled to his heart, causing heart failure.

Bailey Bullock, a student at the John Carroll School in Bel Air, went into cardiac arrest and died after finishing a workout on the high school's track in May 2021. The 16-year-old had a passion for sports, excelled in academics, and volunteered in the community. Though he had a congenital heart defect, he had participated with doctors' approval in previous sports' seasons. He had been granted permission to run track after passing a required athletic physical. His heart failure was possibly triggered by ending his track workout without an immediate cool-down.

I looked back on the deaths of these vigorous, seemingly healthy runners in my community and worried that I too might be a candidate for heart failure. It seemed an irrational fear, as I had no family history of heart disease and had passed recent physicals involving electrocardiogram testing of my heart.

For years, I had felt fit and healthy in my training even though my pace had slowed considerably. But I realized that these local runners who had died may have felt the same way. Wearing a chest-strap heart monitor in my interval workouts on the treadmill gave me some assurance that my heart was responding as it should to these moderate-intensity workouts. But the more I learned about runners' heart failure, the less confident I became in the health of my heart.

World-Class Runners Also Suffer Heart Damage

Accounts of some world-class runners' heart failures worsened my fears. I had watched Peter Snell on television win three Olympic gold medals for New Zealand in 1960 and '64. He set world records in the middle distances with a formidable kick and remained physically active after his international racing days ended. In 1988, at age 49, he ran a masters mile race in Madison Square Garden in 4:53. He won the U.S. orienteering championship in the over-65 age group, and he competed in table-tennis events at the World Masters Games six years after he was diagnosed with dilated cardiomyopathy, a condition in which the heart's left ventricle is enlarged but weakened by thinning walls. This condition led to his fatal heart attack at age 80.

Ron Clarke was perhaps the greatest distance runner of all time. He set 12 world records in one six-week tour of Europe in 1965. In the 1968 Olympics, held in the high altitude of Mexico City, he finished sixth in the 10,000 meters but collapsed unconscious from lack of oxygen. He sustained permanent heart damage in the race and eventually had a heart valve replaced.

Alberto Salazar was a three-time winner of the New York City Marathon. In 1982, he set American track records in the 5,000 and 10,000 meters and won the Boston Marathon in 2:08:51, beating Dick Beardsley by 2 seconds in what became known as the Duel in the Sun. It was a brutal race in which temperatures climbed into the 70s. Severely dehydrated from failing to take water, Salazar, collapsed at the finish and was given six liters of saline solution intravenously. His victory, however, is seen as the turning point of his career in which he adhered to the more-is-better approach to training, running up to 200 miles per week. Fifteen years later, at age 48, he suffered a heart attack while coaching. His heart stopped for 14 minutes before he was miraculously revived.[72]

These tragic endings affirm that the athletic heart is not infinitely durable, not even with the dividends of being constant and faithful in training for many years. Long-term immunity from heart disease does not accrue in proportion to running mileage, certainly not if the heart is abused in overtraining and over-racing. It can beat reliably for a century if cared for properly, or it can be weakened by exceeding its redline redefined by heat injury leading to muscle damage, enunciated by pain, breathlessness, or collapse when stressed.

I had dreamed of becoming like these world-class runners in performance, but I wondered: was my fate instead to eventually suffer heart disease as they did? Was there hidden within me a flaw that would one day be fatal? Would it be a tiny clot that would break loose and lodge in a blood vessel serving the heart, or would there be a gradual narrowing of an artery through atherosclerosis, potentially strangling a portion of the heart muscle to death when called upon to support strenuous exercise.

Dr. Kenneth Cooper's Investigation of Jim Fixx's Death

Such was the fate of Jim Fixx. He had lost a portion of heart muscle to silent heart attacks on the run and ignored the loss of power it caused, probably thinking that running would cure it. It was one factor that led to his fatal heart attack on what was to be a routine 10-mile run one summer afternoon in Vermont.

When Dr. Kenneth Cooper learned of Fixx's death, he felt compelled to explain it to the world. Fixx was the author of *The Complete Book of Running*, which sold over a million copies.[73] As the title implies, Fixx knew all about running. He practiced what he presented in the book, though not completely. That became apparent after July 20, 1984.

In his 50s, he routinely ran 10 miles a day, seven days a week, and on that date in 80-degree heat, he set out to run his usual 10 miler. After only two miles, however, he turned around, probably because of some discomfort, and he ran slowly back toward his motel. He stopped after he had run four miles then collapsed and died of a heart attack on the side of the highway. He was 52 years old.

"Little did I realize the impact Jim's death would have on my life and on joggers and runners all over the world," wrote Cooper. "The press, the media, Jim's followers, non-exercisers, and the merely curious came to me or called from everywhere, and they all asked the same question: How could Jim Fixx die while jogging?"[74]

Cooper is the author of *Aerobics*, and 18 other books which together have sold more than 30 million copies and have been translated into 41 languages. A physician, he coined the term aerobics and established the hugely successful Aerobics Center in Dallas, Texas. He was a miler at the University of Oklahoma a few years before I ran there, and he had, as of age 90, logged over 38,000 miles of running.

He arranged for an exhaustive investigation of Fixx's death to be conducted by his friend William Proctor, an attorney, author, and former reporter. The product of his investigation was *Running without Fear*, a thoroughly researched, well-written book that should be a must-read for coaches and runners of any age. Here are some of the findings about Jim Fixx in the book.

His autopsy showed he had extensive blockage of three blood vessels of his coronary arteries resulting from the buildup of fatty substances.

He had suffered at least three mild "silent" heart attacks, as evidenced by scar tissue on the heart. One occurred two weeks before his death, another four weeks before, and another eight weeks before.

He had been a heavy smoker for years before he started running. Smoking can lead to heart attacks by interfering with the blood supply to the heart.

His lifestyle before he began running was sedentary, and he was as much as 60 pounds overweight before he slimmed down to about 170, just before his death.

His family history was ominous. His father had suffered a massive heart attack at age 36.

His heart was abnormally large, and probably had been so since childhood.

He did not undergo regular, comprehensive medical exams and had never submitted to a maximal stress test. Four years before his death, he had a medical exam in which the electrocardiogram showed significant abnormalities, which were never followed up on.

He had been under a great deal of stress for years.

He had experienced angina chest pain in the previous month.

Running Without Fear was published in 1986. Though I was well aware of Jim Fixx's death when he died, I did not read the book until three decades later, when I was looking for assurance about my own heart's health and durability.

***
The Trigger

One very important finding described in the book is that Fixx likely did not cool down at the end of his fatal run. He simply stopped abruptly. This may seem trivial to experienced runners, who usually delay their cool downs or don't run them at all, but the cool down is extremely important. Done properly it might have allowed Fixx to run another day, although he would not have escaped his fate for long without medical intervention.

"The basic, guiding principle is never stop exercising suddenly," wrote Dr. Cooper. "Don't stand still. Don't sit. Don't stand motionless while taking your pulse. Keep moving, keep moving, keep moving!"

How does failure to cooldown adversely affect the heart? When a runner finishes a race, workout, or strenuous repetition, both the heart rate and blood pressure are very high. They remain high for perhaps 2 to 5 minutes, but in stopping, standing still, or sitting down, the muscle pumps in the legs cease to return blood upward to the heart.

As described in Chapter 20, with inactive muscle pumps, blood settles in the veins of the lower legs and feet, forced downward not only by gravity but also by blood pressure and velocity produced by the pounding heart. The one-way valves in the veins of the legs that comprise the muscle pumps cannot stop the downward flow through the arteries, and the flexible walls of the veins expand to accept the rapidly flowing blood. No longer returning to the heart, a substantial amount of blood collects in the veins of the lower legs and feet and *is temporarily taken out of circulation*. This reduces the flow of oxygen-rich blood to the muscles of the heart and to the brain.

Failure to cool down is thus a trigger for heart failure. After long or intense runs on warm days, it can become a hair trigger when blood volume is reduced through sweating, and blood flow to the skin is increased for cooling. And if there is partial blockage of a blood vessel of the heart, even if it is causing no symptoms, the sum of the decrements in blood flow can reach the point of heart failure.

I checked my own trigger mechanism during an interval workout on the track one day using my chest-strap heart-rate monitor. In running eight repetitions of 100-meter fast runs, each followed by 100-meter walk, I stopped immediately after the last repetition and watched my heart rate drop. In the walking rest interval, my pulse had dropped from 160 to 120 in about 1 1/2 to 2 minutes, but when I stopped abruptly after the last rep, it dropped quickly past 100, then past 90, 80, 70, 60, and 50 at a frightening rate and bottomed out at 40 before I began to walk to bring it back up. It was unnerving. I was seeing how the trigger cut the blood flow to the coronary arteries—but without the heart defect that might have completed a fatal combination.

I visited a cardiologist for the first time in 20 years and submitted to a full series of tests on my heart. The testing was not a confidence-builder, however. The doctor did not understand, though I told him, that I was a long-time runner, and I wanted specifically to know that if after 50 years of interval training I should continue interval training. I wanted to know if my heart was enlarged and if so, was there an apparent decrease in its wall thickness. I told him what concerned me was still experiencing skipped beats, the same type I first noticed 55 years earlier. I said I could feel my heart stretching in my chest after arising in the morning and when walking up stairs in the morning. Was it supposed to stretch so noticeably? I did not remember this happening when I was younger.

He seemed not to consider any of the information I presented to him. I believe it didn't matter to him that I was a long-time runner. He viewed me as any 74-year-old male. Consequently, he prescribed the stress test not as maximal, as Dr. Cooper recommended in his book. It was sub-maximal, apparently for safety reasons, and consequently less stressful than my routine interval workouts. It was, however, a nuclear stress test, and it did show that there was no blockage of the blood vessels of the heart. That gave me confidence, but his review upon first seeing my echocardiogram results, which took him about three minutes to do, did not.

If this testing had uncovered a defect caused by my racing, it would probably have developed in the marathons I ran in stressful conditions.

What built my confidence in my heart was reading *Running Without Fear*. It provides powerful lessons that all runners and coaches should read.

Chapter Twenty-Two
Roger Bannister should have been my role model

Upon turning 60, I received as a gift a copy of *The Perfect Mile*.[75] It was a popular book about three of the world's best milers—Roger Bannister, John Landy, and Wes Santee—competing on different continents to be the first to break 4:00. When I began to read it, I stopped on the second page of the prologue. I then put it on a shelf. Twelve years passed before I picked it up and read it. Why the long lapse of interest? Three sentences:

> *"They spent a large part of their youth struggling for breath. They trained week after week to the point of collapse, all to shave off a second, maybe two during a mile race. There were sleepless nights and training sessions in rain, sleet, snow, and scorching heat."*

I suppose a book prologue is like a movie trailer, amplified in volume to capture potential viewers interest. I saw these three sentences of the prologue as hyperbole, a dose of fiction in the front pages of an otherwise excellent non-fiction book about the competition among three great milers. The three sentences were inaccurate—or imperfect relative to the book's title—in describing elite milers' training.

Having learned the training details of the three, and having run many workouts similar to theirs, I can safely say that not one of these great runners ever reached the point of collapse in a workout. Bannister and Landy trained intuitively much of their careers, enduring the pain of intense fatigue only in races, not in training. If they struggled for breath it was only for a brief period after a hard mile race. When Bannister ran 400-meter repetitions in interval workouts in the six months before he broke 4:00, he ran only 10 repetitions, not 20, not 40, not 100 as Emil Zatopek was known to have done. Most of Bannister's 400-meter intervals were slower than his target race pace for the mile. He ran them at a pace at which he could recover and be ready to run again in 2 minutes. Snow or sleet? Some hard-core fitness runners obsessed with their unbroken daily running streaks might risk workouts in treacherous footing. Not elite runners. They know better.

Having seen over the years many exaggerations in the media about how hard runners train, I thought that the author was trying to sustain a misconception about runner training that has contributed to a life-imitating-art culture of overtraining—that success is forged only by brutally hard work, the more, the harder, the better. Though there is no precise definition for hard work, the workouts middle-distance runners actually need to succeed don't begin to approach the arduous training of professional athletes in other sports, such as the seven hours a day some Olympic swimmers are known to train. Swimmers, by the way, don't have to deal with the damaging effects of eccentric muscle contractions.

The truth is found in physiology: extreme training is not beneficial for runners except perhaps the very rare high responders, the 0.01 percenters like Jim Ryun, who could repair and recover to work extremely hard again a day or two later. Training intensity is limited by each runner's resilience, running economy, adaptability, and durability. This is governed mainly by the susceptibility of leg muscles to damage as the muscle fibers lengthen against force, and the time allowed to repair such damage. The faster the pace and the longer the duration, the greater is the damage and the length of rest required for recovery. The secret to success lies in finding but not exceeding the ever-changing point of optimal intensity, duration, and frequency of workouts.

I should have been more discerning in selecting a role model for the 10 years in which I pursued the sub-4 mile. I chose a sort of composite Ryun, Snell, and Smith as my role model. I should have chosen Bannister, but very little was published about his training. I finally learned the details of his training the year I turned 70, when I read the fortieth anniversary edition of his autobiography.[76]

Bannister might have been considered a contrarian. He usually trained alone and allowed himself only an hour-long workout per day, five days a week. He was always self-coached, though Franz Stampfl advised him regularly during his final year in optimizing interval training. Even before he became a physician, Bannister was keen on science and trained intuitively most of his career; consequently, he became adept at finding his best training intensity.

In his autobiography, he wrote, "ever since I started running I have been trying various methods of training and racing. Each race is an experiment." He sought to minimize the effect of negative factors so that in races, he "would have the spontaneous joy felt as a boy running wildly along the shore."

Like Bannister, I tried various methods to learn how best to train and race, but if I had simply modeled Bannister, I would have shortened my learning curve. His mostly intuitive approach to training produced a steady improvement toward sub-4. It was a natural progression, not forced progression. He did not try to push the river. Though my progression paralleled his for seven years, mine was at times held back by over-training and over-racing. In my self-coached regimen, I only once experimented with lighter training before facing the reality of not breaking 4 minutes. I also did not vary how I tapered for races. I lugged The Bear, it seemed, more often than I ran like a deer.

What Bannister Did Right and I Did Wrong

He tapered for races liberally; for example, he rested actively (working as a physician in the hospital), for five days before his historic 3:59.4. My rest days, mostly inactive in a school or office environment, were too few in my most strenuous periods of training and racing with too much anaerobic running between races.

He raced at most twice per month and did not run more than one race per meet. I applied no constraint over my racing, doubling whenever it seemed challenging or it was needed for team scoring.

He limited his 400-meter repetitions to 10 when running threshold interval training. Mine typically involved 14 to 20 repetitions. I tried sharpening with 4x400-meter high-lactate interval workouts three to four days before a race. This did not work well. It involved too much anaerobic running close to each race.

He had no mileage goals. His training involved only about 20 to 25 miles per week. I usually had mileage goals and ran an average of 55 miles per week in the 10 years I pursued the sub-4:00. I ran many 100-

mile weeks in pursuit of a vague concept—building an aerobic base. I should have cut back on my mileage once my performances plateaued. I did not.

With his training time limited by college studies and medical school, he was always efficient in his workouts, deriving the most benefit possible in the limited time he had for training. "Bannister had time for only about one hour of running five days per week. No long easy jogging before or after practice," wrote Ross McWhirter.[77] I was much less efficient.

He trained intuitively most of his career. I trained empirically most of mine, copying workouts of elite runners who were superior, far more developed than I.

He focused on mile and half-mile races. I became distracted by marathons, half-marathons, 10-milers, and 10Ks, from which it was more difficult to recover; these were not beneficial for achieving my goal as a miler.

His four favorite interval workouts were 15 x 150, 10 x 440, 3 x 880, 2 x 1320. Mine were 24 x 200, 14 x 400, 6 x 800, and 3 x 1 mile.

He took time off to recover from hard races. I did not properly allow for recovery after long road races or doubles in track meets. I went right back to interval training after one day of easy running.

He and I both sought more knowledge of the science of runner training. After seven years of serious training, however, he and I arrived at the same threshold of success, 4:02. With his background in intuitive training and his knowledge of science, he knew how to find his point of balance in workouts, racing, and resting. I did not, and once I plateaued following the 4:02.1, my punishment was to carry The Bear on the final half-lap of every mile race. During that plateau, I could occasionally run like a deer in longer races but my power and running economy necessary for a sub-4 mile, were diminished.

Had I known more about Bannister's training and racing and applied it when I began self coaching, I believe I would have broken 4 minutes.

Then, as Bannister did, I should have drawn the finish line for my competitive career and become a fitness runner of just 12-14 miles per week, as recommended by Dr. Kenneth Cooper.

Chapter Twenty-Three
My long post-racing decline

In topographical terms, my running career began with a steady but gradual uphill climb during which I was buoyed by dreams of a promising future in racing. After seven years on the ascent, I reached a plateau and tried for 12 years with only intermittent success to resume an upward path. I then slowed my pace on a less stressful downward slope 35 years long. The slope was so gradual and the checkpoints—running against the clock—so few that I couldn't see the extent of the decline until I reached my seventies and looked back at my path of descent.

Throughout this period of no racing, I expected to retain much of my speed and endurance in reserve, because I continued to run daily, mixing moderate interval workouts three times a week with comfortable runs of about 4 miles each. This training, I finally realized, was only marginal if I were ever to compete again, even in the lightly-populated over-70 age groups. My well-tuned efficiency which once yielded a high level of aerobic power, anaerobic power, and running economy had gradually diminished. Two checkpoints—a 5K race and an 800-meter time trial—showed that my losses of speed and endurance were much greater than I expected.

I ran my last race at age 41, two years after my tibia fracture on the ice. By then I thought I had recovered well enough to return to road racing. I was wrong. The 5K brought me only disappointment and ended any hopes I held for masters competition. It was an unpleasant experience, not just because it was slow relative to my times of two years earlier, but because it was painful in an unfamiliar way. Though I had been training consistently, it was at less-than-optimal intensity. I began to understand why competitive runners beyond their prime seldom sustain efforts to return to racing .

Twenty-three years passed before another checkpoint, my last one, an 800-meter time trial on the track. At age 64, I had been training daily with interval workouts on a treadmill. This time, I ran behind a pacer who volunteered to help me reach my target of 2:30. I finished in 2:40, which sadly was the pace I could have sustained on a 10-mile training run in my twenties without breathing hard. It was the most painful half mile I ever ran.

Was my performance decline a normal one to be expected by any aging runner? I began an analysis as if I were troubleshooting an old car to be rebuilt into a smooth-running classic. I wanted to determine what parts had failed or were near failure to see what might be salvageable.

Running' performances decline with age at rates determined by many factors. Perhaps the most controllable of these are sleep, nutrition, and a balance of stress and recovery in exercise. When these are not optimal over the long term, the effect of accumulation, I believe, is most important in the decline of conditioning, performance, and health.

The accumulation effects are mainly: (1) the buildup of atherosclerotic plaque in the arteries, (2) the buildup of un-repaired damage to muscle and other tissue resulting from training and racing, and (3) the accumulation of body fat in weight gain.

These differ from losses of *de-conditioning*, which are short term losses. Every runner who takes a break in the off-season gets a feel for these. They involve the reversal of beneficial adaptations. If the losses have occurred over a short period, they can be reclaimed over a similarly short period.

Here, as I perceive them, are the salient elements of my decline from age 40 to 75.

Accumulation Effects on the Vascular System

You are as old as your arteries. This medical maxim—which also extends to capillaries, arterioles, and venules—is mainly about atherosclerosis. This is a disease of aging, and it underlies cardiovascular disease, the leading cause of death in the world.

Atherosclerosis involves a buildup of fatty substances, cholesterol, cell waste products, calcium, and the fibrous material in blood clots. It may begin as early as infancy with fatty streaks, deposits that may slowly increase in size over years to form plaques on the internal lining of an artery. Such plaques can eventually limit or completely block the flow in a blood vessel.

I believe a substantial portion of my decline is due to atherosclerosis in the form of peripheral arterial disease in my legs, mainly the lower legs, and forearms, despite the beneficial effects of a half-century of daily running. This may have had its beginnings in my adolescence before I became a runner, when I had a predilection for ice cream, cheese burgers, pizza, brownies, and whole milk, before I began to take nutrition seriously.

Peripheral arterial disease is known to reduce the circulation not only to the limbs, but also to the kidneys, digestive system, and other parts of the body. Depending on the arteries affected, it can cause many different diseases.

At age 75, my resting blood pressure has been good, but having ideal blood pressure does not mean that all the blood vessels in my body are free of partial or complete blockage, or that the elastic arteries remain elastic. I learned, however, from a stress test with nuclear dye at age 74 that there is no blockage of my coronary arteries. This provides me some assurance that other arteries may be open but could have increased resistance to flow.

Poiseuille's Law of physics informs me that even small constrictions in the arteries could be detrimental to my performance as a runner. This law states that the velocity of steady fluid flow through a narrow tube (a blood vessel) varies directly with the pressure and the tube's radius to the *fourth power*. This means that if the inside radius of the blood vessel is reduced by half, the flow rate with the same pressure from the heart is reduced to one-sixteenth (that is, by 93 percent). That's a huge drop, the significance of which depends on which organ that artery serves.

Atherosclerosis progresses in stages. In stage one there is damage to the inner layer of an artery wall caused by high blood pressure or an immune response to cholesterol that has been deposited in the artery. The second stage is the development of the fatty streak with foam cells formed when white blood cells called macrophages attempt to digest cholesterol, become engorged, and burst.

The buildup can be slowed with lifestyle changes involving diet and exercise.[78]. Can constrictions in the arteries be *reduced in size* with diet and exercise? A well-known clinical trial, the Lifestyle Heart Trial, showed that the constrictions of coronary arteries can be decreased with a low fat vegetarian diet and lifestyle changes including moderate aerobic exercise, mostly walking. Among 20 to 28 patients with moderate to severe coronary heart disease, these changes resulted in a relative improvement (less constriction) of 4.5 percent after one year, and 7.9 percent after five years without the use of lipid-lowering drugs. It was observed that the main determinant of change in percent diameter of the constriction was how well each patient adhered to the specified changes in diet and exercise.[79] The process is apparently very gradual. Conceptually, as the deposits of fatty substances are eroded by the sheer stress of fast-flowing blood, they may move downstream to block a narrower segment of a blood vessel.

In stage three, the plaque grows and toughens and is less likely to diminish benignly. In stage four, the plaque can rupture and produce clots that can break loose, travel downstream, and block blood vessels as they narrow. The effect thus becomes more severe with each stage over time, leading to a heart attack, stroke, failure of another organ, or simply a reduction in a runner's aerobic capacity. It may take years to reach a point of substantially constricting blood flow, but as plaque builds up and a person becomes more sedentary, the rate of deposition of fatty substances may increase.

Research has shown that with the increased velocity of blood flow during exercise, the sheer stress produced by the blood flow is beneficial to the structure and function of the blood vessels. It keeps the internal lining of the arteries smooth to minimize the damaging effects of white blood cells and platelets. In well-trained runners, the flow rate may increase during intense efforts to a rate five to eight times greater than the resting rate.

Curves and branching points are areas of the arteries at which deposition is most likely to occur. This is where the change in direction of the flow reduces the shear stress on the inner radius.[80] It is likely that one's posture when sitting or sleeping with knees flexed at an acute angle can temporarily increase the torturous flow path of arteries, raising the potential for increased deposition.

Increased Body Weight

Weight gain affected my power-to-weight ratio as a runner in two ways. First, more power was required in running when my body weight was 170 pounds than when it was 150. Second, with increased weight, it takes more power and endurance of the muscles below the knee to achieve maximal energy recycling and power amplification.

When I ran my best mile at age 24, I weighed 150. At age 39, I still weighed 152 to 155 at the end of a workout. At 64, however, I weighed as much as 185 pounds, with most of the gain coming in the two years after the broken leg. Even though I had trained consistently and had sufficient discipline about food and beverage consumption throughout the years, I gained about a pound per year.

In my 60s, I began to lose weight gradually with a heart-healthy diet and by 74, my weight had dropped to 165 pounds. What would be the effect of those 10 extra pounds on my time in a mile race? Perhaps only 2 seconds per pound, or about 20 seconds for a mile. That 20 seconds would be significant if I were 24 and racing, but my workouts informed me that my performance drop in my seventies was far greater. It was 3 to 4 minutes per mile.

When he was 49 years old, Peter Snell competed in a masters mile race in New York City's Madison Square Garden . He ran 4:53, almost a minute slower than the world record he set 24 years earlier. He lost 14 pounds to prepare for the race, dropping to 168, the same as his racing weight in his prime. Clearly, it was more than just added weight affecting his performance. His slower time at age 49 was likely due to a loss of aerobic and anaerobic power and running economy.

Foot Mechanics and Achilles Tendons

In my racing days, I experienced delayed-onset muscle soreness in my calf muscles after almost every race, and I typically did not wait for complete healing before resuming strenuous training for the next race. The muscles below the knee are the most highly stressed in racing, and the loss over time of the strength they provide, can result in inefficient foot mechanics, one of the most significant of the accumulation effects.

The faster the pace, the greater is the strength and endurance required to maintain ideal foot mechanics—that is, to keep the heels from dipping, as described in Chapter 15. In my seventies, I could not do this at a pace faster than jogging speed of 9 minutes per mile, a problem likely due to the loss of fast-twitch muscle fibers of the calf muscles. The result was poor energy recycling, power amplification.

I dropped from a good forefoot strike to heel clicking—trying to keep the heels up but failing to do so as indicated by the noise of the heels striking the track. The deficient foot mechanics may also have been partially due to reduced elastic strength of the Achilles tendons, which had been injured years earlier. Diminished elastic strength of these tendons can occur with broken or deformed collagen fibrils of the tendons. Diminished elasticity also occurs with the loss of the titin biological springs within the fast-twitch muscle that is lost.

The Feet

Fat pads on the balls of my feet became thin, making it painful to run downhill without wearing highly cushioned shoes. This caused me to reduce my pace, even at a slow jog, going downhill. Applying too much cushioning, however, causes power losses through energy dissipation in shoes that typically have less than optimal (less than practical) elastic stiffness for returning the kinetic energy of the runner's leaps. My foot arches also weakened over the years. Healthy arches act as biological springs. This is minor relative to the energy recycling by the biological springs of the legs, but arches can weaken to the point of becoming energy dissipators instead of energy savers.

Venous Valves

My left lower leg shows indications that a venous valve may be damaged. Prolonged sitting, which I have done a lot of as a writer in recent years, can make the valves stick in the open position. If blood clots form on a valve, it can allow blood to flow in the wrong direction or to be deficient in pumping power for returning blood to the heart. This condition is indicated by numbness in my toes, by the pain of mild claudication in sleeping on my side with knees bent, by the left leg being slightly weaker than the right, and by slow healing of cuts or scratches on the left shin.

Aerobic capacity

Once I began to train more lightly at age 40, I did not need a maximal oxygen consumption test to determine that my aerobic capacity was diminishing. My basal heart rate, a rough indicator of cardiac power, rose from 45 beats per minute at age 40 to 55 beats per minute at age 75.

Aerobic capacity is said to decline about 1 percent per year after age 30 depending on one's level of physical activity. As would be expected, it declines more in people who become sedentary than in those who remain active and exercise regularly. In ceasing to train as a runner, it diminishes significantly within weeks. In my case, it began diminishing when I quit racing and began training at a lower level of intensity.

One reason for the decline in aerobic capacity is a change in the stroke volume of the heart. The heart stretches, and the stroke volume increases incrementally with each heartbeat when accelerating into a run or walking up stairs. Even while jogging at age 74, real-time readings of my heart-rate monitor upon starting each repetition of an interval workout indicated that stretching was occurring. This was another indicator that my heart was retaining a portion of its peak power. My max heart rate in my seventies has been 165, about 20 beats per minute above what is predicted by my age.

Even if my heart retained much of its power as the training intensity diminished, that alone would not be enough to make me competitive in age-group racing. Aerobic capacity must be developed and sustained on both the supply end and demand end of the arteries. Improving aerobic power requires conditioning the muscles of the power train to extract oxygen and process it at high rates with the fuel stored within the muscle fibers.

Anaerobic power is also increased at the muscle-fiber level by improving the lactate transport within and out of the muscle fiber. To prevent a decline in the metabolic processes of both aerobic and anaerobic power requires faster-paced interval training than I ran during the period of decline. The problem, of course, is that it is difficult for older runners to perform faster-paced workouts without developing leg injuries. By lowering the stress of daily workouts, my aerobic power surely diminished with the shrinking or disappearance of mitochondria, the bacteria-size powerhouses in the muscles of the power train. So too did the other elements in the muscle fibers necessary to produce metabolic power—myoglobin, enzymes, capillaries, lactate-transport molecules, and glycogen storage space. These losses are likely to be at least partially reversible with training, particularly with interval training.

The Lungs

The respiratory muscles decrease in strength as people age, more so in men than in women.[81] In the 800-meter time trial I ran at age 64, my respiratory muscles fatigued rapidly, causing intense pain. Changes to the mitochondria in muscle fibers can occur in the aging process, particularly in decreased enzymatic activity of the respiratory muscles.[82] This could likely have been prevented by increasing the training intensity to gradually rebuild the endurance of the respiratory muscles leading up to the time trial.

The Muscles

In my 70s, I could perceive that my ability to recover from workouts was substantially reduced, as indicated by the post-workout feeling of dead legs that persisted much longer than it did after races in my prime. This lack of resilience could have been due to a decline in the glycogen metabolism and decline in the secretion of hormones such as testosterone, growth hormone, and insulin-like growth factor. Each diminishes with age, but can be sustained with exercise.[83] Aerobic exercise or resistance exercise can delay or prevent the decline in these hormones with aging.

Studies comparing muscle characteristics of older, highly trained athletes to younger athletes have demonstrated that lifelong exercise can maintain and improve muscle function regardless of age. These studies emphasize the importance of continuing to exercise throughout life to reduce the adverse effects of aging and sedentary lifestyle.[84]

Muscle fibers are among the most rapidly regenerable cells in the body. Large numbers of new myofibrils can be generated in days, hastening recovery after a workout, race, or injury. The process of regeneration is conducted by a microscopic committee of cells and hormones essential for building new muscle fibers. Perhaps the most remarkable of these is the repair kit of self-replicating stem cells stored and ready for activation within each muscle fiber. These are known as satellite cells.

The availability of the satellite cells begins to decline as early as age 30, particularly with lack of exercise.[85] Activating the satellite cells with regular exercise is key to minimizing the loss of this capability, which results from the accumulation of cell waste and damage.

Several hormones are important players in muscle maintenance. These signaling molecules initiate and control the process affecting muscle growth and function. They too diminish with aging.

The Kidneys

As a runner, I was always concerned about the condition of my heart, lungs, legs, and feet, but never about the well-being of my kidneys. Out of sight (or touch), out of mind. By age 75, my kidney-concern had grown. The kidneys had lost filtering effectiveness, as blood tests in my physical exams had shown. I was left with about one-third the kidney function I had as a 20-year-old.

Some of this loss was due to normal aging. Some was possibly caused by excessive salt in my diet or by the products of routine muscle damage resulting from the eccentric muscle contractions of running, particularly myoglobin, which normally resides inside muscle fibers and has a direct toxic effect on the kidney.

Kidneys can be damaged by poor blood flow, and running a single marathon can result in acute kidney injury.[86] I was not aware of this when I ran each of my marathons in heat-stressful conditions. I also did not know that running caused a redirection of blood flow away from the kidneys to sustain greater power for running, particularly in racing. The blood flow rate through the kidneys, for example, might drop from 1,100 to 900 milliliters per minute in light exercise and to about 250 milliliters per minute in maximal exercise.[87]

Older runners may also have increased resistance to flow in the arteries serving the kidneys due to atherosclerosis, reducing the flow even further while running. If a runner fails to cool down properly, blood may pool in the veins of the lower legs and feet, further reducing temporarily the blood flow to the kidneys at a time post-race when they are still challenged with a heavy load of waste in the blood. In marathons in hot conditions, the water losses of perspiration can take significant amounts of blood plasma out of circulation.

Sustained high blood pressure can also damage kidneys. Though my resting blood pressure has long been in the normal range, systolic blood pressure while running can exceed 200 mm of mercury, particularly if aging has reduced the elasticity of the aorta. Depending on the power of the heart, this loss of elasticity can prevent the normal smoothing of the pressure pulses from the heart, and possibly make damage to the kidneys more likely in long races.

* * *

Hydration

At 74, I realized I had been in a state of chronic dehydration for about five years. I was slow to recognize this and its significance, not knowing that dehydration—which occurs when one loses more fluid than is taken in—becomes more common in older runners. Among the changes that increase the potential for dehydration is a loss of thirst sensation. I lost my sense of thirst and as a consequence did not drink enough.

Muscle mass is important for storing water. If muscle mass declines along with kidney function as one grows older, the body's ability to conserve water diminishes. I found this true and learned that it becomes difficult to adapt to fluctuating temperatures and workouts in a warm ambience and to control sodium intake with processed foods and restaurant foods in the diet. When performing daily workouts, this makes the task of the pituitary gland and kidney more difficult in controlling electrolyte concentrations, important in maintaining normal heart rhythms.

I have also experienced occasional dizziness and unsteadiness in walking—another result of my difficulty of staying properly hydrated. As water in the body is depleted, the lymphatic flow decreases and the lymph becomes stagnant, congested and dirty due to a build-up of toxins that cannot be eliminated at the normal rate. This worsens some of the symptoms of dehydration—fatigue, dizziness and headache.

Blood volume can drop as a result of dehydration, making even the above-normal power of the athletic heart insufficient for optimal running performance and rapid recovery. Dehydration can also lessen the ability to restore glycogen to the muscles after a workout or race. Restoration of this main energy source for running requires at least 3 grams of water to be stored with each gram of glycogen.

Bones and Joints

My knee, hip, and ankle joints have shown remarkable durability. I believe there are two reasons for this. First, I have maintained good natural foot mechanics for most of my years of running—heels up slightly when the foot strikes the ground toe down at an angle of about 15 degrees. The heels should hover, dropping only about a centimeter so that only the Achilles tendons stretch. Though degraded by wear and tear, my Achilles tendons have served me well for years as shock absorbers, power amplifiers, and energy recyclers. At one point, I was diagnosed with a stress fracture, which occurred after the training hiatus for the broken leg, and for a time I was a heel striker.

The second reason for the durability is that I have been moderately successful in controlling my weight. I have had some minor, transient pain in the joints of the hips, knees, and ankles but no serious injuries. I have known runners who became heel-strikers after many years of running. Some had artificial knees installed, ending their running careers. Artificial knees are suitable for walking but not running.

That's the breakdown of how my speed and endurance as a runner slipped away from age 40 to 75. Many of the changes of decline are irreversible. The most serious and intractable may be those of accumulation, particularly those involving atherosclerosis and cumulative muscle damage affecting the lower legs. Some are surreptitious, like the changes to the heart, and the loss of filtering efficiency of the kidney.

The human body is incredibly complex, with many systems interconnected for efficiency, power, endurance, rapid repair, immunity, and survival. For me, repair was not always rapid enough from day to day, race to race.

Some of the changes discussed here can be reversed through training, but only with intensity appropriate for one's recovery ability, or lack of it, in growing older. The problem is the same as it was in my prime years of running—to balance work and rest, damage and repair, depletion and restoration.

I didn't get those balances right as a young man, and I paid a penalty for that during my pursuit of a sub-4 mile. As an older runner, I had to get them right, knowing that the intensity, duration, frequency and types of workouts beneficial for an older runner are sharply limited. Older runners who try to regain the speed and endurance of youth by training as hard as they trained in their youth are sure to fail. Once it is lost, the ability to run like a deer cannot be reclaimed.

Chapter Twenty-Four

How my running came to an end

One day in my second summer of running, before the running boom began and long before cell phones became ubiquitous, I took a phone call while on a morning run in Lawton's largest city park. In this deserted 300 acres of prairie grassland that morning, there were the usual groups of prairie dogs, but there were no other humans in the park. The telephone in a booth beside a softball field was ringing as I ran by, and no one was around to answer it.

I ignored it. I knew it wasn't for me, of course, so I continued along my 2-mile loop. Fifteen minutes later, however, I passed by the phone booth again, and it was still ringing. An emergency perhaps? Surely not one involving this empty softball field. Out of curiosity, I answered: "hello." A man responded, "who is this?" Reflexively, I said: "no one," not intending to challenge him to guess. But he did guess, astonishing me: "Is this the runner?" I said yes. Then, he explained that he was trying to reach a groundskeeper, who was not there. But with his question, he told me something I might never have known had I not answered.

Having run hundreds of miles solo in the park, seldom seeing anyone else, I had become known as *the runner*, the only person running daily along the highway to the park, around the park, past the prairie dogs on the edge of this city of 100,000. There were no others, running or jogging in 1966. Until I accepted this phone call, I believed I was invisible, unnoticed, except by the security-conscious prairie dogs and a single crow that greeted me most mornings with a dive-bomb attack from behind.

Though I later moved to northeast Texas, then to Maryland, my identity for years remained the same wherever I went: I was *the runner*, the nameless, tireless, regularly appearing, solitary guy on the road shoulder, in the park, or on the high school track. I thought I would never lose this identity, that I would still be *the runner*, training daily and racing in age-group competitions even if I reached my hundredth birthday. I daydreamed about winning all the track events in the over-100 age group of the Senior Olympics. That was my newest vision of the future. I thought I could run my entire life, enjoying the freedom and exhilaration of running like a deer, effortlessly, endlessly, leaving behind those short-striding folks who did not train as assiduously as I did.

What made me believe I could do this were my routine cycles of running and recovery. At age 74, I could not recover from workouts as well as I once could, but I could adjust the intensity and duration of the workouts along with the length of the recovery period. I could emphasize adequate sleep and good nutrition; that is, I could focus on the triad of good health—optimal exercise, sleep, and nutrition. In doing this, I would be able to maintain an exceptional level of fitness for my age.

Another Unexpected Phone Call

Half a century later, as I approached my seventy-fifth birthday, I received another unexpected and unforgettable phone call. This one, which came on a quiet Saturday morning, was from my doctor, who had prescribed a series of blood tests for me two days earlier. The lab results came back with a note of urgency. I was told to go to the emergency room right away, without delay.

I had been not feeling right for more than a year. Always very aware of my body, I understood the messages of aches and pains, which, if caused by exercise, would typically go away with a night or two of good sleep. But for this yet-to-be-diagnosed malady, it was easy to attribute the symptoms simply to getting older.

In the emergency room in Bel Air on March 19, 2022, I submitted to several tests, and at 2 a.m. I was placed in an ambulance and whisked away to the University of Maryland Medical Center in Baltimore.

The preliminary diagnosis in the emergency room was acute myeloid leukemia (AML). My white blood cell count was about ten times higher than normal. AML, I later learned, killed Chris

McCubbins, the Oklahoma State University star I ran against in my second year at OU. He won the Pan American Games steeplechase and competed for Canada in the Olympic Games 10,000 meters. He always beat me easily. In February 2009, at age 63, he was diagnosed with AML. Six months later, despite the best available medical treatment, he was dead. He couldn't beat AML.[87]

Halfway through my eight-day hospital stay, my doctors, eminent in the field of blood cancer treatment, reported on my bone marrow biopsy and told me that I had myelodysplastic syndrome-myeloproliferative neoplasm (MDS/MPN), a rare blood cancer that is incurable but treatable. The treatment is aimed at preventing it from progressing to AML. I was told that I would probably require chemotherapy every month for the rest of my life, but that the median survival to expect, based on my age, was three years. I did not feel like I had a deadly disease, but its characteristic initial symptom, I learned, is that you just don't feel quite right.

MDS-MPN is a disease of the bone marrow, the organ hidden within certain bones that produces white blood cells, red blood cells, and platelets. If a certain mutation occurs, the white blood cells (immune cells) can multiply rapidly out of control. This causes overcrowding of the rigid spaces in which the marrow resides, reducing the quantity and quality of platelets and red blood cells being produced then released into circulation.

When too many white blood cells are in circulation, they attack the blood vessels, causing atherosclerosis at an accelerated rate. They weaken blood vessels, causing capillaries to rupture. These effects can have fatal consequences within months. Atherosclerosis can lead to a heart attack or stroke, and the weakened capillaries along with a deficiency of platelets can result in diffuse bleeding.

Soon I began to see and feel the insidious nature of the disease. I lost most of the sight in my right eye due to a bleed from a weakened capillary. My kidney function plunged. I became anemic. My foot pains worsened. Bruises and rashes popped up as random reminders of my condition. Within eight months, I had been given more than 30 transfusions, most of them for platelets. Chemotherapy did not go well, and my MDS/MPN approached the threshold of AML.

I felt that I had failed, that my many years of running had fallen short on expected health benefit. The thousands of miles of daily workouts I had run apparently resulted in the same susceptibility to chronic disease as any randomly selected old person. I had been running routinely, averaging five or more workouts per week, mostly interval workouts, for 57 years in the belief that I would remain vigorous, fit, and healthy into my eighties or nineties, as my parents and grandparents had. Was this an unreasonable belief?

Opathies

Opathy is a suffix denoting a disease or disorder. My blood cancer was accompanied by a strange opathy. My toes became numb, and my feet were tender and sore, with pain I had never before experienced. I learned that this was probably caused by peripheral neuropathy and that it was made worse by the uric acid in my blood resulting from the cancer treatment. The neuropathy also affected my hands. There was a numbness and an occasional feeling like ants crawling inside my skin —a drive-you-crazy type of tingling that could awaken me from a deep sleep. There were also sharp pains that would randomly come and go. Jogging on the treadmill, even at a slow pace would worsen the foot pain. Norm Macdonald, the famous comedian who died of AML in May 2022, described the pain in his feet as being like walking on shards of glass or through fire.[88]

My other opathy was nephropathy, deterioration of kidney function. The critical ability to filter blood and remove waste products had dropped before my cancer diagnosis and substantially after the diagnosis, possibly due to both the cancer and the medicine used to treat it.

Though most organs benefit from the increased blood circulation running induces, the kidneys do not. The body automatically redirects blood flow away from the kidneys to the working muscles to maximize the power available for running. Ron Clarke, the Australian distance runner who set many world records in the 1960s, died of kidney failure at age 78.

Kidney damage can be repaired if treated soon after it occurs. Did the three marathons in which I became severely dehydrated cause kidney damage that was never repaired? I don't know. I did not monitor my kidney function during or after my racing days.

Some of the great runners mentioned in this book have suffered opathies in their old age, particularly proteinopathy in the form of Parkinson's disease. Two-time Olympic marathoner Kenny Moore was suffering from Parkinson's when he died at age 78. So was John Landy, the second man to break 4 minutes in the mile. Roger Bannister, who became one of the world's leading neurologists after retiring from running the mile, treated hundreds of Parkinson's patients. He was subjected to the cruel fate of developing Parkinson's disease himself. He was diagnosed with it at age 81. In a wheelchair by age 84, he died from complications of the disease at 88.

Other runners mentioned in this book succumbed to other deadly diseases. Wes Santee, who sought to be the first sub-4 miler in 1954, died of cancer at age 78, and Emil Zatopek, four-time Olympic gold medalist, died of a stroke at age 78. Jim Peters, the marathoner who came close to death in the 1954 British Commonwealth Games, died at 80 after a six-year battle with cancer. Leonard Hilton, my friend who was the first Texan to run a sub-4 mile, died of pancreatic cancer at age 52. Tom von Ruden, 1968 Olympian from Oklahoma State University, died of cancer at 73. Bob Day, the 1965 NCAA mile champion from UCLA, died of bladder cancer at 67.

Peter Snell, three-time Olympic champion, died of a heart condition that developed long after he retired from racing. Diagnosed at age 71 with dilated cardiomyopathy, a condition in which the heart's ability to pump blood is diminished because the left ventricle is enlarged but weakened. He was fitted with a pacemaker when his heart could no longer pump blood efficiently. Only about 30 percent of the blood in his heart was being ejected with each beat, much less the the normal 75 per cent.[89] This led to his death at age 80. Cardiomyopathy, a progressive disease with a mean survival time of five years after diagnosis, has been described as a delayed death sentence.

Acute leukemia might also be described as a delayed death sentence. MDS/MPN can be so described too, since it progresses to AML in about one-third to one-half of cases.

How did my many years of running come to this? Why did these Olympians, world-record setters, and national champions, possessors of supremely powerful and efficient cardiovascular systems in their prime, develop these diseases in old age? Why did so many of them not live beyond their seventies? Does training and racing at high levels of competition plant the seeds of chronic disease.

There are of course many factors that determine how and when a person succumbs to chronic or terminal disease. It seems obvious that having a strong cardiovascular system and keeping atherosclerosis at bay with appropriate exercise, nutrition, and sleep can be protective. When I searched, I found that as of 2022, there have been little or no research done on the effects of exercise on leukemia, fewer than there have been for Parkinson's, for example. Several studies have shown physical exercise to be an important preventive against the onset of Parkinson's, crucial to maintaining functional ability or slow one's rate of decline.[90]

It seems apparent that if exercise is to protect against the diseases of old age, it must be performed consistently, continuously, and optimally *throughout life*. It should not end upon reaching 65 or any age perceived to be inappropriate for exercising. There are, of course, limits and limiting factors. Even after years of exercise, adaptations can reverse, and atherosclerosis can take over small or large portions of the 60,000 miles of blood vessels in the body. But even with a youthful, elastic vascular system, the random environmental effects of life can induce microscopic failures like the mutation of a gene in the bone marrow, leading to an incurable disease.

When Chris McCubbins was being treated for AML in 2009, his doctors told him to quit running, probably because the increased perfusion induced by running would cause the leukemia cells to multiply more rapidly. This was before the advent of targeted drug therapy, and if he continued to run, he would be feeding the beast.

Beethoven's Advice and a gift of data

"Don't only practice your art but force your way into its secrets; art deserves that, for it and knowledge can raise a man to the divine."

Written two centuries ago, this advice of Ludwig van Beethoven applies not only to music but to all art and science, and this would include the art and science of runner training. For anyone seeking to achieve better athletic performance or simply to ensure good health, the imperative is to dig deeply into the secrets of the human body, to study and learn how exercise can best induce beneficial adaptations and sustain good health.

Early in my treatment, I began receiving the results of all my blood tests and biopsies directly from the hospital lab without delay. They were sent to me via the internet at the same time they were sent to my doctor, who monitored the results and met with me once a month. This rapid delivery of results was required by a newly enacted federal law, the 21st Century Cures Act. Each test report presented 40 to 50 blood parameters. These were *raw* data, however, listed without explanation, so with this mysterious disease, the reports were sometimes terrifying in delivering results that seemed to indicate my condition was worsening.

In my seventh month of treatment, however, my negative opinion of the instant data changed when I received a report on my second bone-marrow biopsy. The report was dense with medical terminology; I could understand only a small portion of it. But I soon realized I had been given a means *to force my way into the secrets* of this disease—to learn more about it and apply knowledge I had acquired in years of studying the physiology of runner training.

The report described the "cellularity" of my bone marrow, stating that at 90 percent, it was very high. I learned this to mean that the density of platelets, hemoglobin, immature white blood cells, and other cells within the bone marrow was so high that it prevents a large portion of platelets from maturing and entering circulation. I hypothesized and visualized how this might be caused by atherosclerosis, perhaps made worse by two effects: first, white blood cells in high concentrations damaging the inner walls of blood vessels causing an accelerated onset of atherosclerosis. The second possible effect is tortuosity, tight turns of the arteries leading into the bone marrow, which may also increase atherosclerosis, preventing good perfusion of the marrow.

This new information suggested a parallel between marrow and muscle on how diet and exercise can reduce the constrictions of atherosclerotic plaque in the blood vessels of the marrow as has been shown to occur in coronary arteries in the Lifestyle Heart Trial. The hypothesis is that more frequent and somewhat more strenuous walking may result in the reduction of constrictions, greater perfusion, and growth of new micro-vessels in the marrow to reduce cellularity and increase circulating platelet counts.

Transition to walking

When I was diagnosed with MDS-MPN in March 2022, running ceased to be my routine exercise. During my week in the hospital, I walked each day, usually a half mile around the hallways of the eighth floor cancer ward, wearing my GPS wristwatch and pushing the rolling stand of instruments that regulated the flow of an intravenous solution.

Later, I continued to work out at home by walking daily on a treadmill inclined at 6 to 10 percent, 10 to 15 minutes at a time, at a speed of 2 to 3 mph. It was exercise inertia at work. But what I learned about cellularity gave my walking a new importance.

Walking, like running or any other form or aerobic exercise, is like a drug—a broad-spectrum drug of varying efficacy. Self-administered with the *optimal dose* of intensity, frequency, and duration, it can be powerful in recovery and preventive maintenance of the body.

Hippocrates wrote that walking is man's best medicine. Glenn Cunningham, the world record holder in the mile in the 1930s, took a long leisurely walk for recovery the day after each track meet. The Lifestyle Heart Trial showed walking two to three times per week to be beneficial for patients with moderate to severe coronary heart disease.

I hypothesized that a 10- to 15-minute walking workout raising my heart rate to about 125 beats per minute two to three times per day, would increase the perfusion of oxygen rich blood to the marrow; increase the shear stress on the inner walls of the blood vessels to gradually reduce constrictions in arteries in and into the marrow; and induce the growth of new microvessels in the marrow. This seemed likely to reduce the cellularity, bring platelets into circulation, and reduce the percentage of immature platelets.

This was neither a cure nor a primary effect, and it involved much uncertainty. To be sure, the targeted therapy with the drug gilteritinib halting the out-of-control mutations of white blood cells was central to the success of my treatment. Targeted therapy is what was unavailable in 2009 to save Chris McCubbins' life. Its availability in 2022 was what made my walking regimen potentially effective as a supplemental treatment to increase circulating platelet concentrations. The drug's effectiveness, however, was known to be relatively short-lived—for months, not years—before the mutant cells would develop aggressive, drug-resistant clones.

I placed an upper limit on the intensity of each walking workout based on my pulse monitor readings, mindful that the walking increased my blood pressure. Acting on weakened capillaries, this could cause more bleeding like that which damaged the retina of my right eye.

Positive results became immediately apparent. Platelet counts in the bloodstream rose, reaching their highest levels in over a year. The numbers dipped briefly and rose again, but the trend was clearly positive. I continued to tweak the workouts the same way I optimized my interval training workouts for the mile years earlier, and I continued to dig into the science of my disease.

In my pursuit of the sub-4 mile, achieving optimal training was a long, iterative, learning process. Fifty years later, as I faced this new, formidable challenge, I was again in the learning mode, seeking to know how to train and how to live with this disease.

After ten months of treatment, I had hoped to conclude this final chapter in a positive way, worthy of a day-dream headline like those I produced in the privacy of my thoughts on training runs decades earlier, imaginary headlines like: *Blewett breaks 4:00*, or *First-Time Marathoner Wins Olympic Trials*, or *Blewett Outruns Ryun*.

These were not reality, of course, but daydreams were an essential element of my energy source. My training and racing were powered by glycogen and dreams. My most recent daydream headline was: *Former runner demonstrates the benefit of exercise in blood cancer treatment*.

Is it possible? Is it practical? Or are the exercise benefits only temporary or illusory? Will the leukemia cells retake command of my bone marrow to make the walking workouts irrelevant? There is no certainty. The uncertainty does not differ much from what a novice runner experiences when starting to train for an eventual sub-4 mile.

So far, however, my 57 years of running seem to be paying dividends after all. I feel strong and healthy almost every day. I have no need for pain medicine. The miracle drug is keeping my white blood cells under control. I am injury free and walking better than ever, though I would prefer to be running—like a deer.

I don't know where this disease is taking me, but being an assiduous runner for so long has prepared me to handle this journey as well as possible.

In my thirties, I believed that my greatest failure in life had been not breaking 4 minutes in the mile. My perspective then was all wrong, however. *Trying* to break 4 minutes was an endeavor of which I am now most proud. In failing to achieve sub-4, I found success. I studied and learned the science and art of runner training in depth, gave my best effort, and ended my quest with greater knowledge, strength, and will-power than I would have acquired had I quit running after my lone track victory in high school. I developed confidence and self-discipline. Running provided me with a positive attitude, sustained my good health for a half-century, and gave me a small dose of joy each day.

Can I beat the odds in challenging this new adversary? The doctors would remind me that MDS/MPN and AML are incurable. And like racing a mile against an Olympian, world-record holder, or national champion, the challenge is daunting. It is both a psychological and physiological one involving many ups and downs. Do I have the ability, the power to prevail in the long term? I look to the words of Eric Liddell, winner of the 400 meters in world-record time in the 1924 Olympics, as memorialized in the film *Chariots of Fire*:

"I have no formula for winning the race. Everyone runs in their own way. And where does the power come from to see the race to its end? From within."

Acknowledgements

I began writing this book in 2012 with the tentative title "The Science of Running Faster." Eleven years and 300 pages of draft later, after changing course numerous times, I took the advice of my son Dan Blewett and rewrote it as a memoir. When I began to do so, the words flowed rapidly into a 24-chapter explanation of how I learned the art and science of training for middle-distance racing, including what I did right and what I did wrong in my pursuit of a sub-4 mile—and how my performance declined in the 35 years after my last race. Dan, who has authored four books for an audience of young athletes, had a huge effect on this book, including excellent critique and assistance in publishing. My wife Joann; Lucie Lehmann, and Larry Pickett reviewed the book and provided valuable comments and recommendations. I am grateful to each of them in urging me onward, to the finish line.

References

Chapter 1

1. Bannister, Roger. *The Four-Minute Mile,* Fortieth Anniversary Edition. Lyons & Burford Publishers, New York, 1981.

Chapter 2

2. Kenny, W.L., J.H. Wilmore, D.L. Costill, *Physiology of Sport and Exercise*. Human Kinetics, Champaign, IL, 2020.

Chapter 3

3. Bowerman, W.J. and W.E. Harris. *Jogging*. Grosset & Dunlap, New York, 1967.

4. Liebermann, D.E. and D.M. Bramble. "The Evolution of Marathon Running Capabilities in Humans". *Sports Med*. 2007; 37 (4-5) 288-290.

5. R. McNeill Alexander. *The Human Machine*. Columbia University Press, New York, 1992.

6. Moore, Kenny. *Bowerman and the men of Oregon, the story of Oregon's legendary coach and Nike's cofounder*, Rodale, 2006.

Chapter 4

7. Costill, D.L. et al. "Impaired muscle glycogen resynthesis after eccentric exercise". *Journal of Applied Physiology,* 1990. 69:46-50.

Chapter 5

8. Walsh, Chris, *The Bowerman System*, Tafnews Press, Los Altos, California, 1983.

Chapter 6

9. Askwith, Richard. *Today We Die a Little, the Inimitable Emil Zatopek, the Greatest Olympic Runner of All Time,* Nation Books, New York, NY, 2016.

10. Commonwealth Sport. "Jim Peters collapses at end of the marathon in the 1954 British Empire Games. https://thecgf.com.

Chapter 7

11. Shecter, Leonard. Sport Magazine, Feb 1964.

12. Daniels, Jack T. "Running with Jim Ryun: a five-year study". *The Physician and Sports Medicine*, 1974.

13. Martin, W.H., E.F. Coyle, S.A. Bloomfield, A.A. Ehsani. "Effects of physical reconditioning after intense endurance training on left ventricular dimensions and stroke volume". *Journal of the American College of Cardiology*. 1986; 7:982.

14. Gambaccini, Peter. "Bernard Lagat isn't afraid to get out of shape". *Runner's World*, Sep 20, 2012.

Chapter 8

15. Lydiard, A. "Understanding of Approach to Training". Presentation to the USTFF Track and Field Clinic, Astrodome, Houston, Texas, Feb 13-14, 1970.

16. Lydiard, A. and G. Gilmour. *Running with Lydiard*. Meyer & Meyer Sport (UK) ltd, 2000.

17. Snell, P. And G. Gilmour. *No Bugles No Drums*. Minerva Limited, Auckland, 1965.

18. Bowerman, W.J. and W.E. Harris. Jogging: a physical fitness program for all ages. Grosset & Dunlap, New York, 1967.

Chapter 9

19. Van Valkenburg, Jim. "18-year-old Jim Ryun Runs Mile Race in Fast 3:55.8", Associated Press. April 24, 1966.

20. Greene, Bob. "Wes Santee Rates Ryun Perfect Runner." Associated Press. April 24, 1966.

21. Wilt, Fred. *How They Train: half mile to six mile*, Track & Field News, Los Altos, 1959.

22. Daniels, Jack T. "Running with Jim Ryun: A Five-Year Study". *The Physician and Sportsmedicine*, McGaw-Hill. 2:9, 1974.

23. Dill, D.B., S. Robinson, J.C. Ross: "A longitudinal study of 16 champion runners". *J Sports Med Phys Fitness* 7:4-27, 1967.

Chapter 11

24. Kujala U.M., S. Sarna, J. Kaprio. "Cumulative incidence of Achilles tendon rupture and tendinopathy in male former elite athletes". *Clinical Journal of Sport Medicine*. 15(3):133-135, 2005

25. Alexander, R. Mc. *Exploring Biomechanics: Animals in Motion*. Scientific American Library, New York, 1992.

26. "This ain't no county track meet," Onceuponatimeinthevest.blogspot.com, vol. 4, no. 43, June 2, 2014.

Chapter 12

27. Crouse, L. "His strength sapped, top marathoner Ryan Hall decides to stop". New York Times, Jan. 15, 2016.

28. Trail Runner Magazine, "Record-breaking Roadster Ryan Hall Finds New Joy in the Middle of the Pack", www.trailrunnermag.com, March 2017.

29. Brown, Pete. Adolph Plummer RIP 440 World Record University of New Mexico, Onceuponatimeinthevestblogspot.com, Vol 5, no. 117, Nov. 30, 2015.

Chapter 13

30. Nack, William. "Pure Heart". *Sports Illustrated*, June 4, 1990.

31. https://www.sport-horse-breeder.com/large-heart.html

32. Costill, David. *Inside Running: Basics of Sports Physiology*. Benchmark Press, Indianapolis, 1986. (Pg 93.)

33. Maron, B.J. "Structural features of the athlete heart as defined by echocardiography", *Journal of the American College of Cardiology*, vol. 7, issue 1, Jan 1986, pp. 190-203

34. Fagard, R.H., "Impact of different sports and training on cardiac structure and function". *Cardiology Clinics*, 1992 May; 10(2):241-56.

35. Astran, Per-Olof, K. Rodahl, H.A. Dahl, S.B. Stromme. *Textbook of Work Physiology: Physiological bases of Exercise*, McGraw-Hill, New York, 2003.

36. Pelliccia A., B.J. Maron, R. De Luca, F.M. Di Paolo, A. Spataro, F. Culasso. "Remodeling of left ventricular hypertrophy in elite athletes after long-term deconditioning. *Circulation*". *105(8):944-8. 2002.*

37. Smit, Claude, "Interval training", *Run Run Run*, (Fred Wilt), Track and Field News, Los Altos, 1965.

38. Wisloff, Ulrik et al. "Superior Cardiovascular Effect of Aerobic Interval Training Versus Moderate Continuous Training in Heart Failure Patients", *Circulation*. 2007; 115:3086-3094.

39. Benda, Nathalie, et al. "Effects of High-Intensity Interval Training versus Continuous Training on Physical Fitness, Cardiovascular Function and Qualify of Life in Heart Failure Patients". PLoS One. 2015; 10(10): e0141256.

40. Convertino, V.A. "Blood Volume: its adaptation to endurance training," *Medicine & Science in Sports & Exercise*. 1991 Dec; 23(12): 1338-48.

Chapter 14

41. "Ryun: I don't want to talk about it." *Des Moines Register*, April 27, 1969.

42. Bascomb, Neal. *The Perfect Mile*, Houghton Mifflin Co., New York, 2004.

43. Astrand, P.; K. Rodahl; H.A. Dahl; S.B. Stromme. *Textbook of Work Physiology: Physiological Bases of Exercise*, fourth edition. Human Kinetics, Champaign, 2003.

44. Brooks, George A. "The science and translation of lactate shuttle theory", *Cell Metabolism 27*, April 3, 2018, 757-785.

45. Bangsbo, J; T.E. Graham, B. Kiens, and B. Saltin. "Elevated muscle glycogen and anaerobic energy production during exhaustive exercise in man" *Journal of Physiology* (1992), 451, 205-227.

46. Sherman, W.M., et al, "Effect of a 42.2-km footrace and subsequent rest or exercise on muscular strength and work capacity". *Journal of Applied Physiology*. 57:1668-1673, 1984.

47. Cobley, John. Wes Santee Profile, https://racingpast.ca. Oct. 19, 2015.

Chapter 15

48. Skadhauge, E. and T.J. Dawson, (1999) *Physiology*. In Deeming, D. C. (ed.): "The Ostrich – Biology, Production and Health". University Press, Cambridge.

49. Rubenson, J., D.B. Heliams, D.G. Lloyd, and P.A. Fournier. "Gait selection in the ostrich: mechanical and metabolic characteristics of walking and running with and without an aerial phase". 2004, *Proceedings of the Royal Society of London*. B 271, 1091-1099.

50. Stampfl, F. *Franz Stampfl on Running,* eighth printing. Herbert Jenkins, London, 1960.

51. Rodgers, Bill, and M. Shepatin, *Marathon Man*, St. Martin's Press, New York, 2013.

52. Costill, D.L. *Inside Running: basics of sports physiology.* Pg 150. Benchmark Press, Indianapolis, 1986.

Chapter 16

53. Costill, D. L., Thomason, H., and Roberts, E. "Fractional utilization of the aerobic capacity during distance running". *Medicine & Science in Sports & Exercise*. 5, 248–252, 1973.

54. Costill, D.L., G. Branam, D. Eddy, K. Sparks. Determinants of marathon running success, Int. Z. Angew. *Physiology*. 29, 249-254, 1971.

55. Costill, David. *Inside Running: Basics of Sports Physiology*. Benchmark Press, Inc. Indianapolis, 1986. Pg 16

56. Jones, Andrew. "The physiology of the world record holder for the women's marathon". *International Journal of Sports Science & Coaching,* vol 1, no. 2, 2006.

57. Costill, David. *Inside Running: Basics of Sports Physiology.* Benchmark Press, Inc. Indianapolis, 1986. pp. 15-16.

58. Hickson, R.C. and M.A. Rosenkoetter. "Reduced training frequencies and maintenance of increased aerobic power". *Medicine & Science of Sports & Exercise,* Vol. 13, No. 1, pp 13-16, 1981.

59. Wilt, Fred. *How they Train,* Track & Field News Inc., Los Altos, 1959.

Chapter 17

60. Storen, Oyvind; Jan Helgerud, Eva Maria Stoa, Jan Hoff. Maximal strength training improves running economy in distance runners". *Medicine & Science in Sports & Exercise* 2008 Jun; 40(6):1087-92.

61. Moore, Kenny, *Bowerman and the Men of Oregon,* Rodale, U.S.A, 2006.

62. MacDougall, J.D., et al. "Muscle substrate utilization and lactate production during weightlifting". *Canadian Journal of Applied Physiology.* 24:209–215. 1999.

63. Jones, Paul and Theodoros Bampouras. "Resistance Training for Distance Running: a Brief Update". *Strength and Conditioning Journal,* vol. 29, no. 1, pp. 28-35.

64. Docherty, David and Ben Sporer. "A Proposed Model for Examining the Interference Phenomenon between Concurrent Aerobic and Strength Training". *Sports Medicine 2000,* Dec. 30(6); 385-394.

65. Dube, John. J., et al. "Muscle Characteristics and Substrate Energetics in Lifelong Endurance Athletes". *Medicine & Science in Sports & Exercise.* vol. 48, no. 3, pp. 472–480, 2016.

66. Costill, David L., *Inside Running, Basics of Sports Physiology,* pp.24-25, Benchmark Press, Indianapolis, IN, 1986.

67. Craig, B.W, R. Brown, J. Everhart. "Effects of progressive resistance training on growth hormone and testosterone levels in young and

elderly subjects". *Mechanisms of Aging and Development*. 1989 Aug;49(2):159-69.

Chapter 18

68. Wilt, Fred, *How They Train: Vol. I: Middle Distances*, Track and Field News, Los Altos, 1973.

Chapter 20

69. Stegall, H.F. "Muscle pumping in the dependent leg". *Circulation Research*, vol XIX, July 1966.

70. Moore, H.M., M. Gohel, and A.H. Davies. "Number and location of venous valves within the popliteal and femoral veins – a review of the literature". *Journal of Anatomy*, 2011 Oct. 219(4): 439-443.

71. *The Textbook of Work Physiology*, fourth edition, page 160.

Chapter 21

72. Salazar, A. and J. Brant. *14 Minutes: a Running Legend's Life and Death and Life*, Rodale, New York, 2012.

73. Fixx, James F., *The Complete Book of Running*, Random House, New York, 1977.

74. Cooper, Kenneth H., *Running Without Fear*, Transworld Publishers, London, 1986.

Chapter 22

75. Bascomb, Neal. *The Perfect Mile*. Mariner Books, Houghton Mifflin, New York, 2004.

76. Bannister, Roger. *The Four-Minute Mile*, Fortieth Anniversary Edition, Lyons &Burford, New York, 1981.

77. McWhirter, Ross. "The long climb", *Athletics World*, 77, no. 5, 35. May 1954.

Chapter 23

78. Marshall, D., E. Walizer, M. Vernalis, "The Effect of a One-Year Lifestyle Intervention Program on Carotid Intima Media Thickness."

Military Medicine, 176, 7:798, 2011.

79. Ornish, Dean et al. "Intensive Lifestyle Changes for Reversal of Coronary Heart Disease". JAMA, Dec. 16, 1998 - vol 280, no. 23.

80. Wood, N.B., et al. Curvature and turtuosity of the superficial femoral artery: a possible risk factor for peripheral arterial disease". Journal of Applied Physiology. 101:1412-1418, 2006.

81. Sharma, G, and J. Goodwin. "Effect of aging on respiratory system physiology and immunology", *Clinical Interventions in Aging*. 2006 Sep; 1(3): 253-260.

82. Boffoli D., et al. "Decline with age of the respiratory chain activity in human skeletal muscle". *Biochimica et Biophysica Acta.* 1226 (1): 73–82, 1994.

83. Gharahdaghi, Nima, et al. "Links between Testosterone, Oestrogen, and the Growth Hormone/Insulin-Like Growth Factor Axis and Resistance Exercise Muscle Adaptations", *Frontiers in Physiology*, vol. 11, www.frontiersin.org, January 2021.

84. Dube, John. J., et al. "Muscle Characteristics and Substrate Energetics in Lifelong Endurance Athletes". *Medicine & Science in Sports & Exercise.* vol. 48, no. 3, pp. 472–480, 2016.

85. Chen, William, David Datzkiw, and Michael Rudnicki. "Satellite Cells in aging: use it or lose it". *Open Biology*, 2020 May; 10(5): 200048.

86. Mansour, Sherry.G. et al. "Kidney Injury and Repair Biomarkers in Marathon Runners." American Journal of Kidney Diseases, 2017 Aug: 70(2): 252-261.

87. Anderson, K. L. The cardiovascular system in exercise. In H. B. Falls (ed.), *Exercise Physiology.* New York, Academic Press 1968.

Chapter 24

87. MacKintosh, Joe. *Chris McCubbins: Running the Distance.* Gordon Shillingford Publishing, Canada.

88. Geoff Edgers, Washington Post, May 29, 2022, "Norm Macdonald had one last secret."

89. Terry Maddaford. "'Mindful of my mortality'- Snell stopped by

heart disease," *New Zealand Herald*, 18 June 2010.

90. Paillard, T., Y. Roland, and P. Barreto, "Protective Effects on Physical Exercise in Alzheimer's Disease and Parkinson's Disease: A Narrative Review. *Journal of Clinical Neurology.* 2015; 11(3) 212-219.

Made in the USA
Middletown, DE
12 August 2024

59026342R00113